MY MOTHER SAID I NEVER SHOULD

CHARLOTTE KEATLEY

The Royal Court Writers Series published by Methuen Drama
in association with the Royal Court Theatre

ROYAL COURT WRITERS SERIES
First published as a paperback original in 1988 by Methuen London Ltd
Revised and reprinted in the Royal Court Writers Series by Methuen Drama
an imprint of Reed Consumer Books Ltd
Michelin House, 81 Fulham Road, London SW3 6RB
and Auckland, Melbourne, Singapore and Toronto
and distributed in the United States of America by HEB Inc.
361 Hanover Street, Portsmouth, New Hampshire NH 03801 3959

Reprinted with additional revisions in 1989
Reprinted with additional revisions, including a Preface, in 1990
Reprinted 1991 (twice), 1992 (three times), 1993

British Library Cataloguing in Publication Data

Keatley, Charlotte *1960-*
    My mother said I never should.
    1. Title
    822'.914   PR6061.E27/
    ISBN 0-413-65120-7

Printed in England by Clays Ltd, St Ives plc

Preface

I wrote the first draft of *My Mother Said I Never Should* in 1985, when I was twenty-five. I wrote it because I didn't know of any plays about mothers and daughters, although we have hundreds of years' worth of plays about fathers and sons, or sons and mothers. The women in Shakespeare's plays have no mothers. Yet it seems to me that a woman's relationship with her mother, that strange bond of love and jealousy, has a lifelong and unavoidable influence.

I set the play across this century because we have witnessed such enormous changes in opportunities for women between each generation – although many of the desires and stresses for women remain unchanged. I have jumbled chronology because this is not a play about memory, but about the emotional inheritance which impinges on our daily decisions. Likewise the child remains inside the woman, often shouting what the adult refuses to hear. Therefore the child scenes should not be nostalgic or coy; these girls are serious, and out of the public eye they are not 'good'.

I wanted to acknowledge the debt that my generation owes to past generations of women; 'feminism' is too often presented as a preoccupation of university educated women in their twenties or thirties. I learned my 'feminism' from the kind of women who invest their energy, often their whole lives, in other people. The behaviour of mothers shapes a nation as much as governments or wars do; so I would call this play 'political' and I wrote it for mainstage spaces.

I have drawn strength from feeling myself to be part of a wave of about twenty-five significant women playwrights who emerged during the 1980s. Their voices are diverse, their techniques often innovative, and I know of no such flowering of women playwrights in the two thousand odd recorded years of theatre. But the media recorded the decade as having produced no new playwrights and no great state-of-the-nation plays. Even now, not one single play by a British woman playwright has ever appeared on the main stages of our Royal National Theatre. Meanwhile it is plays by women which have drawn the biggest audiences at the Royal Court and have been many of the hits in London's West End throughout the 1980s. I'm sure that the number of women playwrights will continue to grow, as there is evidently a demand for these new voices. *My Mother Said I Never Should* has now been performed across Europe, America, Japan and Australia as have many of these new plays by women.

I spent three years re-writing this play, and am indebted to the director Brigid Larmour for her intellectual and emotional support during this period. My first draft was turned down by the 'new writing' theatres, except for Pip Broughton at Paines Plough, where Debbie Seymour directed a rehearsed reading in 1986. Meanwhile Brigid Larmour read the first draft and understood exactly what I was attempting, to an extraordinary and inspiring degree. We workshopped the play through the invaluable North-West Playwrights Workshop in 1986, and Brigid directed the first production of the play at Contact Theatre Manchester in 1987. I am indebted to the original cast, also to Ken Blakeson, Kirsten Baker, Tony Clark, Nettie Edwards, Bill Hughes and Barbara Pemberton for their comments and support.

The play was produced at the Royal Court Theatre in 1989, and I must thank Michael Attenborough and John Wallbank for their support during further re-writing. Also my warmest thanks to Nancy Coyne and Rick Elice for introducing the play to America, and making me feel welcome there.

The play is not autobiographical. My mother and I have an honesty of communication which encouraged me to write this play. The play is above all a tribute to her, and to Brigid Larmour's gifts as a dramaturge and director.

Charlotte Keatley
August 1990

For

Hilda, Prudence, Susan, Victoria, Nicole
Joan, Jenny, Jane, Michele, Nettie
Judith, Shirley, Nancy
and especially
for Brigid, who made the play happen
and for Mum, who inspires me to communicate,
with love.

My Mother Said I Never Should was premièred at the Contact Theatre, Manchester on 25 February 1987. The cast was as follows:

DORIS PARTINGTON
    Born: Oldham, February, 1900. Engaged 1923, married Jack Bradley
    in Oldham, 1924. (Age 5 in child scenes, as in 1905.)   Joan Campion
MARGARET BRADLEY
    Born: Cheadle Hulme, April 1931. Married Ken Metcalfe
    in London, 1951. (Age 9 in child scenes, as in 1940.)   Jenny Howe
JACKIE METCALFE
    Born: London, July 1952 (Age 9 in child scenes, as in 1961.)   Jane Paton
ROSIE METCALFE
    Born: Hulme, Manchester, September 1971.
    (Age 8 in child scenes, as in 1979.)   Michele Wade

Director and Dramaturg Brigid Larmour
Designer Nettie Edwards

A revised version of *My Mother Said I Never Should* had its première at the Royal Court Theatre, London on 23 February 1989.

The action takes place in Manchester, Oldham and London.

The setting should not be naturalistic. The design should incorporate certain objects which remain on stage throughout, such as the piano in Act One and Two, a tub of geraniums, a patch of wasteground. There are no sofas in this play. The setting should simply be a magic place where things can happen.

In the child scenes, each girl is dressed contemporary to her own generation, in the clothes each wears as a child in the 'real' time scenes, e.g. Margaret wears her Christmas frock, Jackie wears her 1961 summer dress.

There is an interval between Act Two and Act Three.

The solution to the Solitaire game is shown at the end of the play.

ACT ONE

Scene One

The Wasteground, a place where girls come to play.

Enter four girls, each dressed contemporary to her own generation, singing:

My Mother said I never should,
Play with the gypsies in the wood,
If I did, she would say,
Naughty girl to disobey!

ROSIE (*chanting*). What are little girls made of? (*Coaxing* DORIS *to answer.*) Ssh . . .

DORIS. Sugar – and – (*effort*) – spice . . . ?

MARGARET. And . . .

DORIS (*hesitantly*). And?

MARGARET. All Things Nice.

DORIS *squirming, doesn't want to repeat it.*

JACKIE (*can't bear it any longer*). Let's kill our Mummy.

MARGARET. Whose Mummy?

DORIS. Whose Mam? (*Copying.*)

ROSIE. Yes, whose Mum?

JACKIE. All our Mummys if you like?

ROSIE. Who's going to do it?

MARGARET (*to* JACKIE). Dare you!

DORIS. . . . Dare you . . .

JACKIE. We'll all do it.

MARGARET. It's my teatime . . .

ROSIE. How?

JACKIE. I dunno . . . Boiling oil.

DORIS. . . . Dare you . . . (*Repeating.*)

MARGARET. Shut up, baby.

JACKIE. Tell you what –

ROSIE. What –

JACKIE. I've got a penknife. I've been
keeping it for something special.

ROSIE. You pinched it off Jimmy Tucker!

JACKIE. And we'll get some string, and take Mummy down by the railway line where there's
a hole in the fence, and I think you have to put a stake through her heart.

ROSIE. We couldn't do them *all*. (*Pause.*) We haven't got enough string.

JACKIE. Just ours, then. (*Conspiratorial.*) They're not in our gang. Also they don't count
because they're babies. They can do their own Mummys when they're old enough.

MARGARET. Do mine! – I don't like blood . . .

JACKIE. Lucy Parker cut her finger off at school.

MARGARET. I'll be sick.

JACKIE. Only the top bit. (*Pause.*) Like a flap.

DORIS. . . . Flip flap flop . . .

ROSIE (*bends to* DORIS). Do you want us to do your Mum?

MARGARET. She's too young to know.

JACKIE. She's got no Daddy: if we do her Mummy, she'll be an orphan and then we'll be responsible.

MARGARET. Her Mummy's all right – She gave us lemonade. (*Pause.*)

ROSIE. . . . She'll split on us though. Then we'll be outlaws.

JACKIE. Go away, baby.

DORIS *cries*.

JACKIE. Go on. Go home. (*Pushes* DORIS *away.*) Tea? Tea time.

ALL. Tea time. Tea time.

DORIS *goes*.

JACKIE. Piggy.

MARGARET. She'd only cry when she saw the blood. Me, I'm not having any babies.

ROSIE. How d'you know?

MARGARET. I'm not getting married.

ROSIE (*pause. Thinks*). Well it still might grow.

MARGARET. What?

ROSIE. The seed. The baby seed, inside you.

MARGARET. It can't! Can it?

JACKIE *has been arranging sweet wrappers.*

ROSIE. What are you doing?

JACKIE. Voodoo. We need bits of her fingernail and hair and stuff.

ROSIE. . . . She might haunt us . . .

JACKIE. You don't know *anything*, do you.

ROSIE *is subdued.* MARGARET *comes to look.*

MARGARET. What's that for?

ROSIE. Voodoo, you wally.

JACKIE. We're going to have a séance. To call up . . . spirits from beyond the grave.

MARGARET. We do that at school.

JACKIE. Do you?

MARGARET. On Fridays. Take buttercups apart, and count their . . . sta – stay – . . . bits.

JACKIE. Shh! Hold hands. (*They obey.*) You have to repeat after me.

MARGARET.⎫
ROSIE. ⎭ After me.

Lights dim a bit.

JACKIE (*deepens voice*). We call up the spirit of – Granny!

ROSIE.
MARGARET. } We call up the spirit of Granny!

JACKIE. Who died three years ago last Wednesday. And lived in Twickenham. Amen.

MARGARET.
ROSIE. } Amen.

Lights darken.

MARGARET. . . . It's getting dark . . .

ROSIE. . . . What happens now? . . .

JACKIE (*deep voice*). YOU from beyond the grave! Tell us how to kill Mummy!

Lights almost blackout. Silence.

JACKIE. YOU from beyond the grave, tell us –

MARGARET *and* ROSIE *see something, scream and run off.*

Figure of DORIS *now as Gran appears upstage, walking slowly towards them.*

JACKIE. Mummy! Mummy! (*Runs off after the others.*)

DORIS *continues to walk forward, oblivious of above. She removes a dustsheet of World War Two blackout material from a large object which it has been completely covering. It is a baby grand piano.* MARGARET *is crouching underneath it, hidden from* DORIS *by a pile of bedding also under the piano.* DORIS *begins to dust the piano as the lights rise for Scene Two and the wireless begins to play.*

Scene Two

Cheadle Hulme, Christmas 1940. DORIS *is 40.* MARGARET *is 9. The sense of a large front room, with austere decor. No Christmas decorations except for a vase of white, wax Christmas roses with a red bow, on the baby grand piano.*

DORIS *dusts the piano lovingly. The wireless plays George Formby's 'Chinese Laundry Blues'. A pile of bedding is folded under the piano.*

DORIS (*singing along*). 'Oh Mr Wu, he's got a naughty eye that flickers, you ought to see it wobble when he's ironing ladies' –

MARGARET. Knickers.

DORIS. Margaret? Margaret! Where – (*Goes to the wireless and switches it off.*). – Come out!

MARGARET (*from the bedding under the piano, with a doll in her hands*). WHO was that?

DORIS. I have to listen to the wireless. In case Mr Churchill makes an announcement. It is my duty.

MARGARET. Knickers.

DORIS. Margaret. Come Out!

MARGARET. It was Suky.

DORIS *walks around the piano.*

MARGARET (*sings, at first softly*). Suky take it off again, off again, off again, SUKY TAKE IT OFF AGAIN –

DORIS (*pulls her out from under piano by her arm*). Never, never!

MARGARET. Suky! (*Comforts the doll.*)

DORIS. I've told you before!

MARGARET. You've hurt Suky's arm! Torn her dress!

DORIS (*shakes her*). *Will* you listen!

MARGARET (*to the doll*). Suky don't cry. Mummy will cuddle you.

DORIS. I shall have to tell Father.

MARGARET (*pause*). . . . Sorry.

DORIS. Pardon?

MARGARET. I'm very sorry Mummy.

DORIS. Mother.

MARGARET (*pause*). Mother.

DORIS. And you've spoiled your frock. I'd just pressed that.

MARGARET. Haven't! . . . Yes I have.

DORIS. Have you done your practice?

MARGARET (*trying a lie*). Yes. Bits of Chopin and Ten Very Easy Carols.

DORIS *removes carol music from piano and replaces it with a piece of Beethoven music.*

DORIS. You ought to be on Beethoven now, not nursery rhymes. The amount we're paying for your tuition.

MARGARET. You're not throwing them away?!

DORIS. Of course not. They'll go to St. Mark's Jumble. Let me hear Beethoven's Minuet in G, Margaret. Have you washed your hands?

MARGARET *holds out her hands, palms up and then palms down.*

Good girl.

MARGARET *sits down at the piano and starts to play, very shakily, Beethoven's Minuet in G. She sways from side to side.*

DORIS. What on earth are you doing, Margaret?

MARGARET. I'm swaying with passion. Like the fat lady in the Hallé Orchestra.

DORIS. We'll have less passion and more perseverance, please.

MARGARET *resumes playing. Sound of an air raid siren, distant. She plays on.* DORIS *nods to emphasize the tempo.*MARGARET *is still playing, but stumbling. Eventually:*

That will do nicely for this evening, Margaret. I think we shall get under the piano, now. Close the lid.

MARGARET. Next Door have got a proper Anderson shelter.

DORIS (*miffed*). So shall we, presently. Father's been to the Depot but they've run out, had a pre-Christmas rush.

They arrange blankets, a quilt, a stone hot water bottle and a bolster. MARGARET *hangs her Christmas stocking on the piano.*

Help Mother make the bed.

MARGARET. Watch out Suky, here comes a big fat bomb! Wheee! Eeee – oww –d–d–d–d–

DORIS. Margaret!

MARGARET. Well it looks like a bomb.

DORIS. It's a bolster.

MARGARET. I *know*, I – Suky thinks –

Distant rumble of airplanes which continues through the rest of the scene.

S . . . Suky wants a Christmas stocking too. She's not very . . . brave.

DORIS. Put your nightdress on.

MARGARET. Where's my gas mask?

DORIS. Here, see I'll put it by the bolster.

MARGARET. Where will you and Father sleep?

DORIS. In the hall.

MARGARET. Why?

DORIS. I think the ground floor is safest.

MARGARET. Why?

DORIS (*pause*). Sometimes the bombs make the houses shake a little. They make holes in the roof. Nothing will fall on you there.

MARGARET. Except the piano. (*Pause. Quietly.*) Gillian's Mother and Father sleep in one bed, not two.

DORIS. Are you getting into bed? (*Rhetorical: MARGARET isn't.*)

MARGARET. Yes. (*Lights fade from here on. MARGARET gets into bed.*) Suky –! (*She holds the doll tight.*)

DORIS. Tuck you up . . . tuck you in.

MARGARET. Will Father Christmas know I'm under the piano?

DORIS. I expect so – see Margaret, you're a parcel and I'm wrapping you up!

MARGARET. *And* they've got a Christmas tree. Why can't *we* have a tree with candles? Can't we?

DORIS. *Mayn't* we.

MARGARET. Mayn't we.

DORIS. No. Pine needles cause a mess. Besides, candles are dangerous.

MARGARET. Can Hitler see them?

DORIS. You never know.

MARGARET (*impressed*). Does Hitler fly over our house?

DORIS. Have you said your prayers? (*Lights very dim now.*)

MARGARET. No.

DORIS. I'll say night-night then. (*Going.*)

MARGARET. Stay a minute! (DORIS *pauses.* MARGARET *doesn't know how to keep her.*) Do you and Father say your prayers? (*Pause.*) Do you?

DORIS. Father does. I think that does very nicely for the both of us.

MARGARET. Do *you*?

DORIS. I'm saying goodnight now.

MARGARET. Will we win the war?

DORIS. Not if you don't keep quiet and go to sleep. (DORIS *goes to the door.*)

MARGARET. What do you mean? (*Pause.*) Gillian says parts of Manchester there's nothing left, just bricks squashed. She says people get squashed under there. (*Silence.*) Mother? . . .

DORIS. Father will be home soon.

MARGARET (*calls*). Mother – (*Pause.*) Mummy . . . (*Pause.*) What happens when you die?

DORIS (*long pause*). I'll bring you some cocoa presently. (*She goes.*)

The sound of aircraft.

MARGARET. Sssh Suky Ssh! – No, I won't hold you. You ought to go to sleep now, by yourself. You don't need your Mummy to kiss you. You're eight years old.

Lights black out. MARGARET *exits taking the bedding with her.* JACKIE *takes her place under the piano.* DORIS *returns, with a floral overall over her clothes. Lights up bright. Birdsong. A May day, it is 1961.* DORIS *is 61,* JACKIE *is 9.*

DORIS. Jackie? (*Peers under the piano.*) Jackie! What are you doing under the piano?

JACKIE. Seeing what it's like. Mummy says you used to put her to bed under the piano here in the Second World War. And listen to the wireless . . .

DORIS. Margaret says you read a lot of books.

JACKIE. Only 'cos she won't let me watch telly. Daddy does. Why d'you call her Margaret?

DORIS. Because she's *my* little girl. You are always your Mother's child, my Mother used to say.

JACKIE. She's my Mummy.

DORIS. I'm her Mummy.

JACKIE. Yes but she calls you 'Mother'. That's different.

DORIS. How?

JACKIE. Just is. (*Pause.*) You won't tell Mummy about the cup I broke?

DORIS. It was only Utility.

JACKIE. What's that?

DORIS. From the war. (*Pause.*) I'll tell her . . . you've been a very good girl. All by yourself, too. (*Pause.*) We'll go in the garden and break two jam jars presently.

JACKIE. Why?

DORIS. Everything goes in threes. If you break one thing, more is sure to follow.

JACKIE. Is that true?

DORIS. So they say.

JACKIE. Who's they? (*She strokes the piano.*) Why has your bath got feet? This is very old wood.

DORIS. As old as your grandparents. It's the first thing we bought after we got married.

JACKIE. Yes it is a bit old fashioned.

DORIS (*rubs wood*). Classical.

JACKIE (*strokes the white flowers in the vase on the piano*). Are these plastic?

DORIS. No! *Wax.*

JACKIE. Can't you afford plastic?

DORIS. I've had those *years*. Since your Mother was a little girl.

JACKIE. We've got new kitchen chairs with yellow seats.

DORIS. Yes. Your Mother likes all these new formicas, doesn't she. (*Disapproving.*)

JACKIE. When you spill your lunch you can wipe it off straight away. *All* our furniture's new. Poor old Gran. It's all old here, isn't it?

DORIS. It was new once. (*Pause.* JACKIE *contemplates this.*)

JACKIE. Do you know something?

DORIS. What?

JACKIE. I like your old house.

DORIS (*pleased*). You tell your Mother.

JACKIE. Why?

DORIS. Do it for me.

JACKIE (*musing*). We don't have a larder you can hide in, either.

DORIS. We'll make fairy cakes, then we can give Margaret tea when she arrives. (*Pause.*)

JACKIE. Lucy Parker in my class can do the hoola hoop to a hundred.

DORIS. And later on I'll teach you how to say grace, in French.

JACKIE. What for?

DORIS (*holds out her hand*). Come along, let's go and find Mrs Beeton.

  JACKIE *hugs* DORIS. DORIS *hesitates for a second, then bends and embraces* JACKIE.

DORIS. Kiss your old Granny, then.

JACKIE (*kisses* DORIS. DORIS *kisses* JACKIE). It's much nicer here.

  They go off together.

  Lights dim again. DORIS *re-enters, without her overall, dressed as at the beginning of the scene.* MARGARET *is not there, but the doll lies a little way from the piano.* DORIS *carries a Utility ware mug.*

DORIS. Margaret? I brought you some cocoa. (*Sound of planes, distant.*) Margaret? Are you asleep? . . . Dear? (*Silence.*) Well then. You'll just have to drink it cold in the morning. (*She sees the doll and picks it up. Going.*) Can't waste good sugar and cocoa. (*Goes.*)

Scene Three

The Wasteground. A secret place which only girls can get to. Two cats wail like babies.
ROSIE *runs in. She finds the bits of sweet wrapper from the voodoo in Scene One. Arranges them in the pattern which* JACKIE *used. Looks at them for a moment. Picks them up. Scatters the pieces, watches them fall.* DORIS *runs in.*

ROSIE. Mum's got the curse. (*Pause.*) Maybe we did it!

DORIS (*pause*). What curse?

ROSIE. *The* curse.

DORIS. Oh. Yes . . . How d'you know she's got it?

ROSIE. You can tell.

DORIS. How?

ROSIE. Just can. Mum's been cross with me all morning.

DORIS. Well??

ROSIE. Well you'd be cross if you'd been cursed. (*Pause.*) Like in that story. She might turn into something.

DORIS. Will she die?

ROSIE. You have the curse until you're an old, old lady.

DORIS. Then what?

ROSIE. Then it stops. (*Pause.*) *Then* you die.

DORIS. Did she prick her finger and bleed?

ROSIE. Dunno. She might've, but I didn't see any blood.

DORIS. Cross your heart she's got the curse?

ROSIE. And hope to die. (*Lowers her voice, conspiratorial.*) We were in the A.B.C. having buns. Mum said she was going to the Ladies. When she came back, she said, 'We'd better go quickly, I've got the curse'. (*Pause.*) So I went into the Ladies to have a look . . . and, sure enough, on the wall, there it was!

DORIS (*frightened*). What?

ROSIE. The little heart-shaped drawing!!

Stunned silence.

DORIS. Oooh . . .

ROSIE. I thought she'd been looking different. Sort of oldish in her face.

They savour the moment. Then, fast.

ROSIE.
DORIS. } Doctors and nurses!

DORIS. Bags be nurse!

ROSIE. I'll be doctor. (*Pause.*) Who'll be patient?

DORIS. All right. I'll be patient and you be doctor and then it's my turn.

ROSIE. I've brought our kit.

ROSIE *opens a plastic carrier with rattling objects inside it.* ROSIE *takes out a large sanitary towel and fits it over her head, with the loops over her ears.*

ROSIE. Good morning Mrs Bradley what seems to be the trouble can you take your knickers off please.

DORIS. I don't think we ought.

ROSIE. You been telling?

DORIS (*pause*). No.

ROSIE. You have.

DORIS. I think Mam knows. What we do . . .

ROSIE. How, dummy?

DORIS (*pause*). She says she can see inside my head.

ROSIE. We'll just have to pretend, then. (*Coughs.*) Can you lie down please not very nice for the time of year is it.

DORIS *hesitates, lies down.*

ROSIE. Tut tut tut.

DORIS. Is it very bad?

ROSIE. I'll just have to feel it.

DORIS (*jumps up*). Don't touch!

ROSIE. But you like it.

DORIS. I might catch a babby.

ROSIE. I think you've got one already.

DORIS. That's my husband's fault, you can't trust him.

ROSIE. How is your husband?

DORIS. Oh he's upped and gone.

ROSIE. Oh I am sorry.

DORIS. I'm not. You must drop by for a cuppa. That's enough now, your turn.

They swap positions: DORIS wears the sanitary towel, ROSIE lies down.

ROSIE. Will you have to stethoscope me?

DORIS. Oh yes all right. (*Takes a kitchen funnel from the carrier bag and listens to ROSIE's stomach.*)

ROSIE. Can you hear anything?

DORIS. Yes I think the babby's coming out.

ROSIE. Shall I tell my husband?

DORIS. No not yet. There's no cause for alarm.

ROSIE. Will it hurt?

DORIS. PUSH! It's like doing a big poo. Then the babby pops out.

ROSIE. You know the yellow nightie we hid? Mam wore that when I was born. It's got a dark red stain on it.

DORIS. It's not, it's brown.

ROSIE. Blood dries up. When it's very old.

DORIS. Truly? Let's go and look.

ROSIE. When a baby's born they cut the cord.

DORIS. What's that?

ROSIE. It joins the baby to its mummy.

DORIS (*contemplates*). Let's be babbies tomorrow.

ROSIE. No, it's weddings tomorrow.

DORIS. Why?

ROSIE. You have to get married first.

Scene Four

Rayne's Park, London, May 1969. The garden of KEN and MARGARET's suburban semi. JACKIE is nearly 18, wears flared jeans with sewn-on badges; MARGARET is 38, wears a flowered apron and carries a tea towel. JACKIE has her red transistor which blares, 'All You Need is Love'. She sprawls on the grass beside the cherry tree, next to the swing. MARGARET follows flustered.

MARGARET (*switches off the transistor*). I should never have let you go to that party in Hammersmith!

JACKIE. Please, Mummy, leave me alone.

MARGARET. You said you were staying with his parents!

JACKIE. We were. But they didn't mind us sleeping together. Not everyone has your hang ups.

MARGARET. Oh you can wound me sometimes, Jackie!

JACKIE. You sound like Granny now.

MARGARET. What am I going to tell Daddy?

JACKIE. If you want me to behave like an adult, then stop treating me like a child!

MARGARET (*pause*). You don't know what might happen.

JACKIE. I might fall in love.

MARGARET (*trying to ignore this*). You can get pregnant the first time, you know.

JACKIE. Thanks for telling me now.

MARGARET. Well if you'd come to me and said –

JACKIE. Well I did say I wanted to have a talk with you, actually, and you said 'Tell me while we go round the garden centre', don't you remember? (*Slight pause.*) Anyway, you can't scare me, because I'm on the pill, OK?

MARGARET. Since when?

JACKIE. Since before Neil and I went away at half term. You knew that because you've been reading my diary.

MARGARET (*momentarily caught*). Well I've no idea, you might be on drugs, anything! (*Collects herself.*) I know I'm going to sound like an old fuddy duddy, . . . but . . . (*Stuck.*) It's a serious step you've taken, you've no idea –

JACKIE. It was no big deal. It was a relief to get it over with. I cried afterwards. Then I laughed. I expect it's better with someone you're in love with.

MARGARET. You could have waited.

JACKIE. Why?

MARGARET. I had to.

JACKIE. That's it, isn't it? (*Gets up and goes to the house.*)

MARGARET. If this affects your A-levels!

JACKIE (*stops*). What?

Silence. MARGARET *has nothing to say.*

JACKIE. I'm going to make a phone call. Phone Neil. (*Goes into the house.*)

MARGARET (*pause. Picks up* JACKIE's *transistor*). I had an admirer. He took me to dinner. I'd never eaten oysters before. – Wouldn't let me see the bill, that sort of man. I was sure Ken could tell, when I got in. I'd had my hair done, on a Wednesday. (*Pause.*) Ten years ago.

Blackout.

Scene Five

Cheadle Hulme, Manchester, 1961 as in Scene Two. JACKIE *is 9,* MARGARET *is 30,* DORIS *is 61. The garden. Sound of lawnmower off right.*

DORIS *enters with a chair and a rug, and arranges them on the grass. She glares, off right.*

DORIS (*calls to right*). Jack! JACK!

The lawnmower sound stops.

DORIS. Are you coming to have tea with us? Ken and Margaret can't stop long.

Pause. The lawnmower sound starts up again. She shouts.

Well you'd better do round the front, I don't want grass clippings in our tea. (*As the lawnmower fades away to right.*) And mind my lily of the valley! (*She goes back to the house for the tea tray.*)

Enter JACKIE *leading* MARGARET *by the hand, followed by* DORIS.

JACKIE. And I've been doing the pear tree. Look. (*She shows* MARGARET *the painting.*)

MARGARET. Oh that's lovely darling!

JACKIE. Grandad let me use his real paints.

DORIS. He's been teaching you, hasn't he.

JACKIE. Did you know shadows are purple?

DORIS. Have you said hello properly?

JACKIE (*hugs* MARGARET). Are you better?

MARGARET. Better? (*Looks at* DORIS.) Mother . . .

JACKIE. Where's Daddy?

MARGARET. He's gone to fill up the car with petrol.

DORIS. That chair's for you.

MARGARET. No, really.

DORIS. The rug will do quite nicely for me. (*Sits.*) Sit down and have some tea.

MARGARET. Oh we mustn't, I said to Ken we'd be ready to leave as soon as he comes back.

DORIS. Her bag is packed and in the hall.

MARGARET. If we stay for tea we won't get home to London till way past Jackie's bedtime.

JACKIE. I don't mind.

DORIS. Jackie made the cakes. Didn't you dear?

Pause. MARGARET *gives in to pressure and sits.*

MARGARET. All right Mother. And what have you been doing, darling?

JACKIE. I broke a cup and then we broke two jam jars.

MARGARET. Oh dear.

DORIS. Jackie's been an angel.

JACKIE (*offering the cake*). Have the yellow one with the smartie.

DORIS. I hope you've been taking the iron tablets, dear.

MARGARET (*resists temptation to answer back. To* JACKIE, *for the cake*). Thank you.

JACKIE (*says grace in French, very fast*). Que Dieu benisse nôtre pain quotidien. Amen.

Pause.

MARGARET. Well this is very nice.

DORIS. And how was Windermere? Did you drive about much?

MARGARET. We stayed in a lovely guest house, a bit pricey but Ken insisted I was pampered.

JACKIE. What's pampered?

DORIS. Nursed.

Pause. JACKIE *looks at* MARGARET. MARGARET *looks at* DORIS.

MARGARET. No, pampered is – being spoiled a bit – like you've been, here!

DORIS. Thank you, Margaret.

MARGARET. And I brought you some Kendal mint cake! (*Gives it to* JACKIE.)

JACKIE. And some for Granny? Never mind Granny, we can share this. (*Breaks it in half and gives half to* DORIS, *then goes back to her painting.*)

DORIS. I hope you didn't do too much walking.

MARGARET. It rained a lot. Luckily there was a nice lounge with a fire. Time to sit and think. You know, Mother, I thought I didn't want it, till I lost it. (*Pause.*) It's been a blessing, you taking Jackie for the week. But I missed you, darling!

JACKIE (*goes and hugs* MARGARET). I cried the first night, didn't I Granny, then at breakfast Grandad let me have your old napkin ring.

MARGARET (*holds her*). Oh Jackie.

JACKIE. And your doll. It's like a real baby, it's got real curled up toes and fingers. I was practising. I bathed it and put it to sleep, and it shut its eyes.

MARGARET. No! (*Gets up.*)

JACKIE. Mummy –

DORIS. Jackie – (*Catches hold of her.*)

JACKIE. I didn't break her, I didn't break the doll!

DORIS (*comforts*). Ssh ssh –

JACKIE. You're hurting! (*Breaks free and runs off, knocking the paint pot across the painting.*)

DORIS. If you hadn't been so hasty to get that temping job, you would never have lost the baby.

MARGARET (*busying herself with the painting*). It'll dry in the evening sun, it'll be all right.

DORIS. That's for Jack. He wanted something from his grandchild.

DORIS *takes the painting.*

Blackout.

Scene Six

A council flat in Mosside, Manchester, early December 1971. JACKIE *is 19¹/₂,* ROSIE *is 3 months,* MARGARET *is 40. A worn piece of rusty red carpet with ashtrays and mugs strewn on it, also the red transistor from Scene Four, now worn and battered, blares out over* ROSIE's *crying. A Moses basket of blankets represents* ROSIE; *the actress playing* ROSIE *can be seen making the sounds of the baby crying. As the lights rise,* JACKIE *is packing baby clothes into a holdall.*

RADIO (*Manchester DJ*). . . . Today's highest temperature is expected to be a cold 3°, so wrap up warm. Most roads in the city have been cleared now, but there's still ice and snow on the Pennines, and the forecast is more snow tonight. Police are asking motorists leaving Manchester on Northbound routes to drive slowly because of black ice. Meanwhile, here's something to remind you of summer days . . . (*'Honky Tonk Woman'.*)

JACKIE (*packing hurriedly*). I wanted it to look nice and now it won't all go in!

ROSIE *yells.*

JACKIE (*hits transistor, which goes off*). Ssh, Rosie, please –

ROSIE *yells.*

JACKIE. Shut up!

ROSIE *stops crying abruptly.*

JACKIE (*gently*). Ssh, ssh, there now . . . Where do you get the energy from, yelling all night? (*Bends over Moses basket, sings haphazard tune.*) My little rabbit, in your little basket . . .

ROSIE *coos.*

JACKIE. Sleep, beautiful . . . ssh . . .

ROSIE *makes a little cry as* JACKIE *moves away to pack again.*

JACKIE (*bends over* ROSIE *again*). Please don't be crying when Mummy and Daddy arrive! – Where's your red sock? (*Picks it up and dangles it over* ROSIE, *who quietens during:*) Look, it fell out! Give me a smile – yes! There. I even washed your red sock. Washed everything, don't want Mummy to think – (*Holding back tears.*) I've got to clear up, Rosie. – All these ashtrays, Sandra and Hugh last night, they never think about you, do they? (*Picks up ashtray.*)

MARGARET (*from off*). Hello?

JACKIE. Oh shit, the mess – Come in!

MARGARET (*entering*). Hello Jackie.

JACKIE (*immediately casual*). Hi Mummy.

MARGARET. It's not locked!

JACKIE. I knew it would be you.

MARGARET. You've been smoking.

JACKIE. Journey from London OK?

MARGARET. Not how I remembered, Mosside. All these tower blocks . . .

JACKIE. Is Daddy – he's not –

MARGARET. Waiting in the car.

JACKIE. He didn't mind? – I'm sorry, I couldn't face –

MARGARET. He understands.

Pause.

JACKIE. This is Rosie, Mummy.

MARGARET. I – came up the stairs. (*Pause.*) Lift is out of order. (*Pause.*) Lot of stairs.

JACKIE.   . . . Please.

MARGARET (*long pause*). Three months.

JACKIE. Say hello.

MARGARET (*goes to the Moses basket. Pause*). Pretty.

JACKIE (*goes also*). You think so?

MARGARET. You had curly eyelashes like that.

JACKIE (*pleased*). Did I?

MARGARET. Hello Rosie . . . (*Kisses her.*)

JACKIE. Don't wake her!

MARGARET. Of course not!

JACKIE. I'm sorry, it's just –

MARGARET. You think I don't know?

ROSIE *coos quietly.*

MARGARET (*very tenderly*). Ssh, there now.

ROSIE *murmurs.*

JACKIE (*turns away*). I've packed her things
 . . . here. (*Gives* MARGARET *the holdall.*) And her bottles are in this carrier. There's a bit of powdered milk left –

MARGARET. Oh you really don't need –

JACKIE. Well what would I do with it?

Awkward pause. MARGARET *looks through the clothes in the holdall.*

MARGARET. I've been to Mothercare. Got some of those new disposable nappies, like you said. Quite different from when you were a baby. (*Sees another carrier, goes to pick it up.*) What about this bag – what a sweet – won't she want this dress with the rabbit on?

JACKIE. Leave those! – Things she's grown out of.

MARGARET. Why did you have to try! All by yourself? Didn't you believe me?

JACKIE. I wanted to see if our theories worked . . . (*Pause.*) But when I came back from hospital everyone had cleared out. You'd think I had VD, not a new baby.

MARGARET. He should be here with you, your – (*Stuck for word.*) – Rosie's father. – You in these flats . . .

JACKIE (*calm*). Mummy, I told you. He visits; and sends money. It was my decision.

MARGARET. Yes but you had no idea! I told you, I told you! Nothing, for nearly three months, nothing, since the day she was born, then a phone call, out of the blue, the potatoes boiled dry!

JACKIE. You knew I'd phone, one day. (*Slight pause.*)

MARGARET. Look at you now, a year ago you had everything, you were so excited about the art school, new friends, doing so well –

JACKIE (*angry*). I'll go back! Yes I will, finish the degree, I won't fail both things! Only think about her at night, her cheek against mine, soft and furry, like an apricot . . .

ROSIE *makes a snuffling noise in her sleep.*

JACKIE. . . . She'll be happy, won't she? . . .

MARGARET. After you phoned . . . after you asked us . . . Daddy went upstairs and got your old high chair down from the attic. (*Pause.*) Like sisters, he said. A new little sister . . . (*Bends down to* ROSIE.) Aren't you, precious?

JACKIE (*panics*). Mummy – she's got to know – I can't come and visit, with her not knowing, I can't!

MARGARET. Jackie, darling, we can't go over this again – you know as well as I do it would be impossible –

JACKIE. I don't believe you!

MARGARET. When she's grown up, you can tell her; when she's sixteen.

JACKIE. It'll be too late!

Silence.

Give me back the bags.

MARGARET (*gently*). You've got such opportunities.

JACKIE. Expectations.

MARGARET. Yes!

JACKIE. Yours.

MARGARET. You've got to –

JACKIE. Why? (*Pulls away holdall.*) Why not just Rosie?

MARGARET. You've got to go further than me – and Rosie too. (*Quietly.*) Otherwise . . . what's it been worth?

JACKIE (*pause*). Here, take them. (*Gives* MARGARET *the bags.*) You haven't told Granny and Grandad?

MARGARET. Not yet. I'll talk to them. (*Tentative.*) – Perhaps you could stay with them, just till Christmas, while you find a new flat? . . . (*Bends to* ROSIE.) My little lamb . . . What's this?

JACKIE. She has to have a red sock to go to sleep.

MARGARET. You keep one.

JACKIE (*puts one sock in her pocket*). Love her for me . . .

MARGARET *picks up the Moses basket.*

JACKIE. I'll help you to the car.

MARGARET. It's all right, Daddy will be there. (MARGARET *picks up the bags. As she goes to the door.*)

JACKIE. I'll come for Christmas. And visit, lots. (*Pause.*) Whenever I can afford the fare to London.

MARGARET *exits.*

JACKIE (*calls after them*). Sing to her at bathtime, especially the rabbit song . . . (*Silence. Pause. She picks up the bag she told* MARGARET *to leave. As she pulls out the clothes, she is suddenly hysterically happy. She holds up the rabbit dress.*) – Wore this the day you first smiled, you wouldn't let go of my hair, – do you remember?! (*Holds up another.*) – And your first bonnet . . . (*Gentle.*) And the shawl . . . wrapped you up, like a parcel, the day we left hospital; all the way back in a taxi, bringing you home . . . (*Pause.*) Our secrets, Rosie. I'll take care of them. (*Pause.*) You'll never call me 'Mummy'. (*Silence. Screams.*) Rosie! Come back! – Mummy, Mummy!

Blackout. For a moment in the darkness, the sound of a baby crying. In a dim light we see MARGARET *rocking a bundle. She comforts the baby with the following words, until the baby quietens and coos:*

MARGARET. There now, there now, hush! Did you have a nasty dream? My precious. Mummy's here now. Mummy's here, Rosie. There now . . . Did you have a bad dream, Jackie? It's all right. Ssh . . . ssh . . .

As the lights come up bright for the next scene, MARGARET *turns and billows out the sheet which was forming the bundle.*

Scene Seven

Cheadle Hulme, Manchester, 1951. A hot August day. A distant rumble of thunder. DORIS *wearing a sensible beige skirt, and* MARGARET, *wearing ski pants, are in the garden folding a single bed sheet. One more sheet remains on the line and one of* JACK's *shirts. Socks lie on the grass, one maroon one a little way off. The rest of the washing is already folded and in a washing basket.* DORIS *is 51 and* MARGARET *is 20.*

DORIS. I'll be glad when they put an end to clothes rationing. These sheets are quite threadbare in the middle.

Sound of light aircraft going overhead.

DORIS (*studies the sky*). R.A.F. from the base at Padgate.

MARGARET. They're B29s, not Lancasters!

DORIS. I'll be glad when they're gone. (*Disdain.*) Americans.

MARGARET. Mother! Without them we couldn't have won the –

DORIS. Are you going to help me fold this sheet, or are you just going to stand there all afternoon identifying aircraft!

MARGARET (*staring at the sky*). Maybe one of them's Ken.

DORIS (*they hold the sheet by the corners and tug*). I don't see how it can be, if he's calling in half an hour.

They shake the sheet vigorously.

MARGARET. I can't wait to live in London! (*No reply.*) Ken says he can get a job there. He's frightfully clever.

They balloon the sheet up into the air.

MARGARET. I'm in love, Mother.

Distant rumble of thunder. DORIS *looks up at the sky.*

DORIS. It's not going to hold. (*Pause.*)

They pull diagonals to stretch the sheet.

MARGARET. And I'm going to learn to type! Ken says it will be helpful if we need a second income. (*As they shake the sheet.*) Typing's far more useful than all those stupid school certificates. I'll get a *proper* job.

DORIS. What do you call running a home? (*Looks up at the sky.*) I knew we were in for a storm.

MARGARET. I'm not wasting my life.

DORIS (*angry*). Thank you Margaret! (*They fold the sheet lengthwise.*) Pull! (MARGARET *pulls so hard that* DORIS *lets go and they jerk back from each other.*)

DORIS. There's no need to snatch it out of my hands! There see, now you've spoiled it all.

MARGARET. Well you can pick it up again, can't you! (*Pause.* DORIS *picks it up, they resume folding.*) I'm not going to have a family, babies and all that. Ken and I have decided.

DORIS (*distant rumble of thunder*). It will break, soon.

They fold the sheet lengthwise.

And what makes you so sure you can keep Mother Nature at bay?

They close in chest to chest and MARGARET *gives her corners to* DORIS, *who folds the sheet in half and half again during.*

MARGARET (*grandly*). There's THINGS you can get . . . I've heard about them.

DORIS. I'm not talking about that. (*Cradles folded sheet.*) I'm talking about the *desire* . . . for little arms reaching up and clinging round your neck. (*She buries her face in the sheet, then holds it out to* MARGARET *to do likewise.*) Smell: lavender. From the beds, there. Mother Nature is very hard to fight. It's not just a question of rubber things or what have you.

MARGARET. 'Little arms clinging' . . . There, see, that's what I don't want. That's the difference between our generations, Mother.

DORIS. Well I'm glad to know you've worked it out, Margaret. Can you sort out Father's socks, please?

MARGARET (*picking the socks off the grass and pairing them*). You want a nice snapshot for the family album don't you? Proof, to show the neighbours. Well I'm going to be different! Women did so much during the war: there's nothing to stop us now.

DORIS. Ha!

MARGARET. You think I'm being selfish, don't you?

DORIS. I felt a few drops, then. (*Pause.*) What makes you think I wanted children?

MARGARET. Mother!

DORIS. I had a job once too. I know it was only teaching, but . . . (*Pause. To stop herself.*) there's an odd maroon one over there, on the grass. (*Pause. Warning MARGARET.*) Of course, Father has absolutely no idea. One would never . . . tell him. (*Pause.*) There wasn't any choice, then; so I don't know whether it was my need – to love him, if you know what I mean . . . or his desire – for a son. (*Long pause. DORIS bends and picks up a sock.*) Horrible colours he likes. Not my choice, maroon . . . Not my choice at all. . . (*Pause.*)

MARGARET. The garden is always so lovely, Mother. May I take a cutting, off one of your geraniums, to London with me?

DORIS. Oh Margaret . . . why does it have to be London? (*Sound of raucous car horn, which repeats.*) Oh I do wish people wouldn't do that! Brings down the tone of the neighbourhood!

MARGARET. It's Ken! He's bought an Austin Healey – it's got a folding roof – you must come and see! I said to honk and I'd move Father's car into the garage so Ken can back into the drive – I'll have a lot of cases to load into the boot.

DORIS. That nice Graham Next Door. All those trips he took you on, to the ornamental gardens at Bellevue.

MARGARET. Yes, Mother. Well I'm *not* going to be a Manchester dentist's wife.

DORIS. I must say, Jack asked my mother before there was any talk of weddings.

MARGARET. Have you still got your posy?

DORIS. He's reversing straight into my lily of the valley!

MARGARET. He's not.

DORIS. He is.

MARGARET. He's not, just parking.

DORIS. Curious method of parking.

MARGARET. That's typical, you think all Americans are brash and wear loud check shirts and chew gum and want to marry English girls. You're just prej– . . .

DORIS. Margaret, that's enough! (*Pause.*) After all, he is going to marry an English girl.

MARGARET. Oh Mother, don't look at me like that with your lips pressed together.

MARGARET *exits.*

DORIS *folds the remaining sheet and puts it in the basket during this speech:*

DORIS. Well it's too late now. These sheets are damp. I knew this lovely summer wouldn't last. (*Pause.*) I suppose I should get the best service out, for tea. (*Rumble of thunder, close.*) She'll need bed linen. These are all worn out . . . Something old, something new. So they say.

DORIS *picks up the basket of washing and starts towards the house. Crack of thunder, overhead.* DORIS *drops the basket, which spills everywhere. Immediately, the sound of pouring rain on leaves.* DORIS *stands and contemplates the spoiled washing all around her as the pouring rain grows louder. Lights fade slowly to blackout.*

Scene Eight

The Wasteground. ROSIE *skipping, chants.*

ROSIE. Georgey Porgy pudding and pie,
    Kiss the girls and make them cry,
    When the girls come out to play –

JACKIE (*runs up, one hand behind her back.* ROSIE *stops.*) I went to the boys' den.

ROSIE. You said you wouldn't!

JACKIE. Only slightly.

ROSIE. You're out of the gang.

JACKIE. I got the penknife back.

ROSIE. I don't believe you.

JACKIE (*takes the penknife from behind her back and holds it out between them*). So there.

ROSIE. So what.

JACKIE. I kissed a boy.

ROSIE. You didn't!

JACKIE. I did.

ROSIE. What's it like?

JACKIE. I think I'm in love.

ROSIE. How d'you know?

JACKIE. Because this boy made me cry. Daddy makes Mummy cry and she says it's because she loves him. (*Opens penknife blade.*) Now we can do the Vow.

ROSIE (*backing away*). It's too late. You've probably got his seed now and it'll grow and grow and fill you up.

JACKIE. You're still my best friend.

ROSIE. Don't talk to me about best friends because I'm never playing with you again.

JACKIE (*pause*). Kissing wasn't as good as best friends.

ROSIE. Why d'you do it then?

JACKIE. To get the penknife.

ROSIE (*pause*). You didn't need to kiss a boy. You could have given him some bubble gum.

JACKIE. I did. He wanted a kiss as well. (*Pause.* JACKIE *holds the blade up.*) They said I'm a cissy.

ROSIE. You are.

JACKIE (*holds up index finger and ceremoniously jabs the tip with the penknife. Studies it*). I'm bleeding.

ROSIE. Do I do it too?

JACKIE. Yes.

ROSIE (*takes the knife and stabs her own index finger*). Ready.

They face each other and hold fingertips together and recite.

ROSIE. ⎱ Truth is honesty
JACKIE. ⎰ Honesty is true,
        Keep your promise
        And I'll keep you.

They step back and suck their fingers; JACKIE puts the penknife away.

ROSIE. You can't ever lie to me now. (*Pause.*) Can you see into the future?

JACKIE (*frightened*). A bit.

ROSIE. Will you have a look for me?

JACKIE (*pause*). It'll happen anyway. Mummy says don't cross bridges.

ROSIE. Is that a spell?

JACKIE. I don't know. She just says it.

ROSIE. At night?

JACKIE. I heard her say it to Daddy, in the garage.

Pause, they look at each other.

ROSIE. ⎱ Don't-cross-bridges!
JACKIE. ⎰

ROSIE. It must be a spell.

Blackout

Scene Nine

Telephone conversation, early December 1971, later on the same day as Scene Six.

MARGARET *in Raynes Park, London, aged 40.* DORIS *in Cheadle Hulme, aged 71.*
MARGARET *dressed as for Scene Six, with the Moses basket beside her.*

DORIS. Hello?

MARGARET. Hello?

DORIS. Margaret?

MARGARET. Mother? Oh, I was just about to ring you. It's not gone six has it?

DORIS. Two minutes ago. We've just got the news on.

MARGARET. Oh dear . . . I'm sorry, I was just seeing to . . . (*Distant ROSIE cries.*) . . . to Ken.

DORIS. Is he poorly again?

MARGARET. Oh, no, no! Well, a slight cold. Very slight.

DORIS. *You* don't sound too well.

MARGARET. I'm fine.

DORIS. You don't look after yourself, dear.

MARGARET (*pause*). Mother, why did you ring?

DORIS. Oh, just to see if you were all right . . .

MARGARET. How did you know?

DORIS (*matter of fact*). What, dear?

At the same time ROSIE *cries in the distance again.* MARGARET *puts her hand over the receiver and collects herself.*

MARGARET. How's Father?

DORIS (*pause*). We've still not seen Jackie.

MARGARET. She's been . . . since when?

DORIS. Well it's been a year, now.

MARGARET. I've only seen her – slightly . . .

DORIS. I suppose she's busy with her studies.

MARGARET. Oh yes, very.

DORIS. Only your Father and I thought she might visit, being in Manchester herself now. She's not moved?

MARGARET. Well, yes, I'm not sure . . .

DORIS. It was Jack's birthday last week.

MARGARET. Didn't you get the cards?

DORIS. Yes, very nice. (*Pause.*) But he usually gets a hand-painted one from Jackie.

MARGARET. Well . . . you know how it is, she's got to rebel while she's still a teenager.

DORIS. What?

MARGARET. Revise. She's got to revise, for her exams.

DORIS. We thought we might go and visit her.

MARGARET. Oh no! I shouldn't . . . just yet. She's decorating, decorating her new flat.

DORIS. She should have asked us. I've plenty of furnishings put by that I don't need any more.

MARGARET. How's Father?

DORIS. Oh, creeping, creeping. Can't do anything with his hands now of course. A mither he was in, trying to sign the will.

MARGARET. You said.

DORIS. So I sold his painting things. Some of those easels he's had since we were first married.

MARGARET. Mother! Why didn't you tell me? Not the sable brushes?

DORIS (*pause*). No. Jack wants Jackie to have them. (*Pause.*) Of course I said to him I don't suppose she'll want those, being at a Polytechnic. (*Pause.*) He sets great store by her, you know.

MARGARET. I'd like you to come and visit us.

DORIS. We're coming at Christmas. Or don't you want us this year?

MARGARET. Of course Mother! I thought perhaps the week after next . . .

DORIS. What is it?

MARGARET. I can't explain on the phone.

DORIS. You're not hiding anything from us?

MARGARET. No!

DORIS. Good or bad dear?

MARGARET. What? Oh. (*Long pause.*) Good. (ROSIE *cries, distant.*) Very.

DORIS. It's not that sofa you were telling us about?

MARGARET. No, it's . . .

DORIS. Well that's two minutes dear. I'll finish now.

MARGARET. Yes.

DORIS. Father will be so pleased to know . . .

MARGARET. What?

DORIS. About Jackie.

MARGARET. What?!

DORIS. Revising for her exams. I'm saying goodnight now.

MARGARET. Goodnight. (*The line has already gone dead.*) Jackie, what are you doing to me . . .?

Blackout on MARGARET *and* DORIS.

Scene Ten

The garden of KEN *and* MARGARET's *home in Rayne's Park, London, as in Scene Nine. Distant jingle of icecream van. September 1979.* ROSIE *is 8.* JACKIE *is 27,* MARGARET *is 48. The cherry tree has grown, the swing is as in Scene Four. It is* ROSIE's *eighth birthday. Enter* ROSIE, *carrying an old spoon and* MARGARET's *doll Suky from Scene Two. It is a baby doll, now bald except for a few tufts which have been spiked.*

ROSIE. It's my birthday today and it's all gone wrong already. I'm going to bury you, Suky. Eight is too old for dolls. I want a Sex Pistols tee shirt. Some hope. Unless Jackie brings me one! I'd have buried you ages and ages ago, Suky, if you hadn't been Mum's. I couldn't care less now if Mum sees me doing this. (*Digs in the tub.*) Suky. Stupid name. Even cutting your hair off it won't go punk. I bet Mum cuddled you and stuff, didn't she? Well I only hug people when I want to, not when it's visitors. (*Holds doll over her face. Pause.*) When I want to I can hug harder than anyone. In the world. (*Pause.*) I'm saving it. (*Pause. Digs hole. Lowers the doll over it, then holds it closer to her.*) I was going to give you away to the Toy Collection at School, d'you know that? Mummys give their babies away sometimes. They do. (*Pause. Slowly lays the doll in the hole.*) Shut up crying. There, see, I'm putting you in this urn. People get buried in urns. (*Covering the doll over with earth.*) Jackie'll be here soon. She never cries. No one else at school has a sister who's a grown-up. I might easily run away with Jackie and live with her. Then you'd be sorry, Suky. So would Mum. (*Suddenly bright, as if enormously relieved.*) I'm going to paint the cherry tree now. – for Jackie.

ROSIE *lies on the grass painting.* JACKIE *enters with a very lavish birthday cake and candles.*

JACKIE. Happy-birthday-to-you! . . . Rosie?

ROSIE. Why did you buy me one? Mum usually makes me one.

JACKIE. Thanks.

ROSIE. I mean, it doesn't look as good as this. And she always makes chocolate because she thinks I like it.

JACKIE. Why don't you tell her you don't?

ROSIE. Oh you know Mum. Never listens. I think she just likes making birthday cakes. Even *Dad* gets one!

JACKIE. Let's light the candles.

ROSIE. Shouldn't we wait for Mum?

JACKIE. Oh, yes.

ROSIE (*pause*). Has it got drink in it?

JACKIE. Rum. A bit.

ROSIE. Mum and Dad never drink anything exciting. You know that funny shaped bottle you brought them from Mexico? It's still in the cabinet.

JACKIE. Well I brought Mum some Greek lace this time. Sort of thing she wouldn't treat herself to.

ROSIE. She's so *mean*! D'you know, she wouldn't even buy me a Sex Pistols tee shirt, she says 'No dear, you haven't grown out of last year's summer dresses'. As if I could be seen wearing those!

MARGARET (*enters with a tray*). What's that dear? Here we are, celebration drinks! How long is it since you were last here, Jackie?

JACKIE (*silence*). I don't know. Light the candles Rosie.

ROSIE (*as she lights the candles*). One . . . year . . . and four months.

MARGARET. I thought we'd have some of the tequila you brought us, Jackie. We keep it for special occasions.

JACKIE (*to* ROSIE). See.

ROSIE. Me too?

MARGARET. A little bit.

Pause. All three watch the candles burn.

MARGARET. Magic.

JACKIE. I used to wish . . .

MARGARET (*cuts in*). Blow the candles out.

ROSIE. I think Jackie wants . . .

MARGARET. Now darling, before it spoils.

A moment while ROSIE *hesitates.*

MARGARET. Blow the candles out.

ROSIE (*blows the candles out*). Done it! (*Pause.*)

JACKIE. Wish, Rosie!

MARGARET. No, you hold the knife and wish as you cut it . . .

JACKIE. No, you wish *first*!

MARGARET. No, Rosie and I always . . .

ROSIE. Oh stop it, you two!

MARGARET. Don't we, Rosie. (*Silence.*) *I'll* cut it then. It must have cost Jackie a lot.

ROSIE. I don't want any now. (*Gets up.*)

JACKIE. Don't go. What's this, Rosie love?

ROSIE. You mustn't look! I can't paint like you can!

JACKIE. It's lovely, Rosie.

ROSIE. 'S not, the sun's running down into the grass.

JACKIE. It could be abstract, all swirls.

ROSIE. Don't be stupid! It's a mess, even you can see that.

JACKIE. Can I keep it?

ROSIE (*snatches it away*). It's for Mum. Here, Mum. (*Gives it to her.*) It's gone wrong.

MARGARET. It's lovely! Thank you, pet. (*She and* ROSIE *embrace.*) Say sorry to Jackie.

ROSIE. Sorry, Jackie.

   JACKIE *is watching intently.*

MARGARET (*looks at the painting*). Where shall we put it? The kitchen walls are choc-a-block.

ROSIE. On the fridge.

MARGARET (*laughs*). Run and put it there, before someone sits on it, like Daddy did.

   ROSIE *exits. Awkward pause.*

MARGARET. How's Manchester?

JACKIE. Fine.

MARGARET. Working hard?

JACKIE. Yes. (*Uneasy silence.*)

MARGARET. I've got a full-time job now, too.

JACKIE (*pleased*). That's good. I'm hoping to open a gallery of my own in a couple of years, with Simon, if we can get the backing.

MARGARET. Oh I did like Simon.

JACKIE. We're not – together any more.

MARGARET (*gently*). It would be nice, Jackie, if you found someone, I know you'll hate me for saying this, but it could be very lonely when you're –

JACKIE. Mummy – (*Stops.*) Simon wanted children, I tried to believe I could start again. – Stupid – I just kept dreaming about Rosie.

   Moment.

ROSIE (*calls*). Mum! – Where's the Blu-tack?

MARGARET (*calls*). In the cupboard with the carrier bags.

ROSIE (*calls*). Oh, s' all right . . .

JACKIE. She doesn't need me, does she?

MARGARET. No.

ROSIE (*running in*). No what?

MARGARET. No you don't ride your bike on the main road.

ROSIE. I do! Me and Zoe Taylor nearly crashed, we were kazooming –

JACKIE. Well you shouldn't! NEVER, ever – I'm sorry Rosie, I didn't mean to shout at you –

(ROSIE *has run off. Silence.*) I do worry about her getting run over, or getting ill, or lost or attacked, and me not being there . . .

MARGARET. I worry about YOU.

JACKIE. Still?

MARGARET. Mothers don't grow out of it.

JACKIE (*hands MARGARET a small carefully wrapped package*). Here.

MARGARET. A present – for me? (*Opens it.*)

JACKIE. It's lace.

MARGARET (*turning it over in her hands*). Where was it you were this time? – Greece? (*Bemused.*) I try to imagine what it's like, when you go off on these trips by yourself, no one else to think about!

JACKIE. It's from the convent on the island. The nuns have used the same pattern for a thousand years.

MARGARET. Thank you dear.

JACKIE (*slight pause*). Mummy, I've been given a rise; new bikes are expensive . . . I want to give you a cheque –

MARGARET. How dare you! This isn't one of your art deals! (*Snatches the cheque and tears it up.*)

ROSIE (*runs in*). What is it Mum? (*Hugs MARGARET. To JACKIE.*) I hate you! (*Clings to MARGARET.*) Mum, I want you to see where I've put my painting.

MARGARET (*as they go into the house together*). . . . . All right darling.

JACKIE *stays sitting a moment. She sees the old spoon and scattered earth, then goes to the cherry tree in its tub, digs out the doll which* ROSIE *buried, brushes it down. It is naked except for one red sock.* JACKIE *takes the other red sock from her pocket. As she puts the sock on the doll the lights fade to blackout, so that as she raises the doll to her cheek she is only just visible.*

Blackout.

ACT TWO

Cheadle Hulme, Manchester, December 1982. The large front room of DORIS *and* JACK's *house. A french window to the garden and a door to the hall. Dustsheets over boxes and the piano. Snow on a rose bush outside the window.* DORIS *is 82,* MARGARET *is 51,* JACKIE *is 30,* ROSIE *is 11.*

ROSIE (*enters with a flashlight, swings it round. Pause.*). Grandad? You in here? (*Silence, listens.*) Well if you're listening, I want to tell you that it was pretty stupid, what you did – I mean, leaving the house and stuff to Jackie. Mum and Gran were mega hurt, you know that? (*Pause.*) Grandad . . . ? I'd like to know, did you do it because you like Jackie best . . . or because you're jealous? (*Silence. Listens. A rustle.* ROSIE *jumps, swings the flashlight round.*) Mice. (*Pause.*) I'm not scared of you, Grandad. It's the others who are. You didn't get me. (*Switches off the flashlight and goes out to garden through french windows, shutting them behind her.*)

Enter JACKIE *carrying boxes and binliners. She puts these down and exits.*

MARGARET *enters with a bag and rubber gloves, guiding* DORIS.

DORIS. Two months ago Saturday Jack died, and the house hasn't been aired since.

MARGARET. Well we can soon put that right, Mother.

DORIS. I doubt it.

Lights on suddenly and bright. DORIS *startled.*

JACKIE (*re-enters*). I turned the power on, and the water.

DORIS. Oh I don't think that'll be necessary.

MARGARET. Mother we have to see to clear up.

JACKIE. You don't have to worry about bills now, Granny, I've worked it all out. (*To* MARGARET.) I've backed the van up the drive so we can load things straight in.

DORIS. My lily of the valley!

JACKIE. I couldn't see. There's snow over everything.

DORIS. It was terrible on the motorway driving up.

JACKIE. Have you had a good time in London?

DORIS. . . . Terrible . . . (*Still referring to the journey.*)

MARGARET. Yes well we're here now, Mother. Have some tea, I've brought a flask. (*Gets out the thermos and pours a cup.*)

DORIS. I'm quite all right. You have some.

MARGARET. I want to get on.

JACKIE. Sit down while the house warms up.

DORIS. I don't want to be a nuisance to anyone.

MARGARET (*wavers, cup in hand*). Jackie?

JACKIE. Got sugar in it?

MARGARET. Yes.

JACKIE. You know I don't.

MARGARET. You've got no sense of compromise, have you?

ROSIE *knocks on the French windows with a white rose.*

MARGARET. Look at Rosie.

DORIS. She'll catch her death.

MARGARET. She never does. (*Lets* ROSIE *in.*)

ROSIE. Look what I found! (*Looks like one of the wax roses in the vase on the piano in Act One, Scene Two.*)

MARGARET. A Christmas rose.

DORIS. It's dead.

JACKIE. It's not, it's frozen.

ROSIE. That's dead.

JACKIE. We could unfreeze it.

ROSIE. Even you can't organise roses to come alive.

DORIS (*going to French windows*). They should all have been pruned by now . . . all blown down by the storms.

ROSIE (*pulling* DORIS *away from the window*). C'mon, we can't prune them now.

DORIS. I don't want whoever buys this house to think Jack and I didn't know about roses.

JACKIE (*trying to please*). We can pay to have the garden done, before we sell.

DORIS (*stiff*). All that money, and Jack would never spend a penny of it.

ROSIE. Mum, can Jackie and I make a snowman?

MARGARET. Rosie we've only got today and tomorrow to get this house sorted out. I don't suppose Jackie wants us in her flat any longer than that.

JACKIE. Mummy, you can stay as long as you like, you know that!

MARGARET. You said you've even been using your bedroom to store paintings.

JACKIE. That was before the exhibition. Anyway Rosie's room is always ready.

ROSIE. Mum, can't I stay –

MARGARET (*sharp*). Rosie. (*Pause.*) Now Jackie, you tell us all where to start. Seeing as Father left you in charge of everything.

JACKIE. Come on Mummy, that's only because I live in Manchester too. He knew I'd be on the spot to deal with the house.

MARGARET. I suppose being born in this house doesn't count, Jackie. (*Beat.*)

JACKIE (*passing a binliner to* DORIS). Granny, you take a binliner and –

DORIS. She's going to put it all in dustbins!

JACKIE. You choose which curtains you'd like from this room, the rest we'll leave for the auction.

MARGARET. I'll make a start on the crockery, then. (*Pulls dustsheet off a set of shelves. A willow pattern service is on the lower shelves, ornaments and framed photographs above.*)

ROSIE. Okay don't talk to me.

MARGARET. Rosie, bring that box over and start scrunching up newspaper for packing.

ROSIE (*kicking the box over to* MARGARET). Do some chores instead.

JACKIE (*goes over to the dresser*). I'm sure you'll want to keep the willow pattern, won't you Granny?

DORIS. Old. Cracked.

They wrap and pack the willow pattern during the following dialogue.

MARGARET. Mother, you sit tight and we'll pass you things to wrap.

DORIS. I shan't want any of this. Jackie's possessions now, according to the will.

JACKIE. Granny, you'll need things for the house in Oldham.

DORIS. It's not a house. It's an End Terrace.

ROSIE. Come off it Gran, that's a bit mean. Jackie bought you exactly the house you wanted.

MARGARET. Rosie! Don't be rude.

ROSIE. Well I think you're both being rude to Jackie. She can't help what Grandad did.

DORIS. It seems that sixty years of housewifery counted for nothing, in Jack's eyes.

MARGARET. Your house has always been a gleaming example to us, Mother. Rosie, can you fetch some more newspaper please.

DORIS. Well Jackie didn't follow it, did she. (*Slight pause.*) Jack noticed *her* sort of work, because he was always asking how her painting exhibitions were going. And since Jackie didn't care to visit much, I had to make it up. And as you know, modern art was never my strong point.

ROSIE. She hardly ever visits us, Gran.

JACKIE. – I'm always there for your birthdays, Rosie.

ROSIE. Most of them.

JACKIE. I try –

ROSIE. S'okay Jackie, you have to travel lots, and your work's the most important thing, isn't it. (*Pause.*)

MARGARET. Funny how a job was never a good enough excuse for me. I think Father disapproved of it.

ROSIE. But your job's only typing, Mum. (*Slight pause.*) Anyway, Jackie's different, she's got no kids. (*Pause. One mug left at the back of the shelf.*)

ROSIE. What's this vile mug?

DORIS. That's Utility, Rosie. I used to give Margaret cocoa in that.

MARGARET. I'd forgotten.

ROSIE. Mum's always giving us cocoa.

MARGARET. It's funny, Mother, Jackie and Rosie don't even like cocoa.

DORIS. You only want what you're denied.

ROSIE *passes mug to* JACKIE, *who wraps it.*

JACKIE. Oh yes – I broke the handle once – see where Grandad glued it?

MARGARET. I don't remember.

JACKIE. Oh – you weren't here.

MARGARET. Whyever not?

JACKIE. Well it was the summer you – (*Stuck.*) – weren't well.

MARGARET (*pause*). I don't remember.

Pause. JACKIE *puts the mug in the box which is now full and tapes it closed.*

JACKIE. There's the willow pattern, Granny.

DORIS. That was my wedding. Was never the set I wanted.

Pause.

JACKIE. Rosie, take Granny into the kitchen and see if there's any pans she'd like to take.

DORIS. What about the bedrooms?

MARGARET. What about them, Mother?

DORIS. Well Rosie will need bed linen.

ROSIE. What for?

DORIS. You never know.

ROSIE. I've got a duvet.

MARGARET. Rosie.

ROSIE. I have!

JACKIE. Rosie, why don't you and Granny go upstairs and sort out some sheets.

DORIS. Come along, princess.

ROSIE. I'm not a princess. I'm a punk. – We could get in your old wardrobe, Gran.

DORIS. Why, love?

ROSIE. 'Cos it's brill for hiding. – Come on Gran.

As ROSIE *leads* DORIS *out of the room.*

DORIS. I want to know, when did I stop being Granny, and turn into Gran?

ROSIE. You like it.

Pause.

JACKIE. I thought we might have a chat.

MARGARET. We can while we finish these shelves, can't we.

JACKIE *does not reply. She fetches the stepladder and puts it by the shelves.*

JACKIE. How's work?

MARGARET. Fine. How's yours?

JACKIE. Oh – okay. (*Pause.*) I'll climb, and pass you things.

They work.

MARGARET. I read an article at the hairdressers, about a girl who does silk-screen printing, in Sheffield. Rather like you.

JACKIE. I don't do silk-screen printing. (*Pause. Passes a frame.*) What a serious child you were!

MARGARET (*looks at it*). On the beach at Scarborough. I was six years old. I remember Father wanted a nice one . . .

JACKIE. 'The highest standard', he'd always say to me.

MARGARET. 1937. I remember Father kissing me that day, and saying, 'You're nearly grown up now.' He didn't kiss me after that. (*Pause.*) If you left a bit of butter on your plate, it was either Mother on at you about rationing, or Father would tell us again, how he started his business with a tin of boot polish, cleaning gentlemen's shoes on the steps of the Royal Exchange. What that had to do with butter, I really don't know.

JACKIE (*lifts down a silver rose bowl*). The rose bowl. 'Manchester Business Award, 1949'.

MARGARET. He took me to the Exchange once, to look at his shares. Young women had to wait outside, of course. (*She has a spasm of pain.*)

JACKIE. Mummy – is it upsetting you? – Sit down for a bit.

MARGARET (*fighting pain*). So much to do. (*Continues packing.*)

> JACKIE *looks worried.*

> Next shelf, Jackie.

JACKIE. The pottery duck I made – look.

MARGARET. Rosie made that.

JACKIE. No, I made it for Grandad.

MARGARET. I think I should know.

JACKIE. Mummy I –

> MARGARET *has another spasm of pain.*

> Please stop doing things for a moment.

MARGARET. It's just menopause. Cramps . . . (*She sits.*)

JACKIE. It shouldn't do that to you. Have you seen a doctor?

MARGARET. Surgery hours are nine till six. I'm working then.

> *Pause.*

JACKIE. Rosie's very energetic . . .

MARGARET. She's like you.

JACKIE. . . . I meant it Mummy, about school holidays.

MARGARET. And how would you cope, the hours you work?

JACKIE (*pause*). I could time share with Sandra at the City Art Gallery. I asked her. – She's got two small children now.

> *Pause.*

MARGARET. All Rosie's schoolfriends are in London.

> *Pause.*

JACKIE. It was just an offer. (*Clumsily.*) If you ever feel you can't cope –

MARGARET. What are you suggesting?!

JACKIE. Mummy, I want to ask you – (*Stops.*)

MARGARET (*pause*). What?

> *They look at each other. Long pause.*

JACKIE. Let's get on.

> MARGARET *gets up,* JACKIE *climbs stepladder.*

> When I've sold this house and invested the money for everyone, you won't have to work so hard.

MARGARET. I have to work. There's always something. I don't have your attitude to the future, Jackie.

JACKIE (*pause.* JACKIE *at top shelf*). That's everything. – No, what's this? (*Lifts down an old chocolate box. Opens it.*) – Look, a Victorian photograph! The frame's made of shells . . .

MARGARET (*pause*). That's mother's mother.

JACKIE (*excited*). Is it? Look at that stiff black dress – and the high collar.

MARGARET. Goitre. Women over thirty never showed their necks in those days. Swellings. Hormone problem. No proper medicine to control it.

JACKIE. Why hasn't Granny ever showed us this?

MARGARET (*pause*). Jack didn't like it. (*Pause.*) Mother grew up in what she calls – reduced circumstances . . . Her mother wasn't married.

JACKIE – *stunned.*

I found out in a letter once.

JACKIE (*fury*). How could you?

MARGARET. What?

JACKIE. Never tell me!

MARGARET. It wouldn't have made any difference, Jackie.

JACKIE. You know it would! (*Angry tears.*) Mummy –

A moment. JACKIE *can't speak. Suddenly* ROSIE *bursts into the room with a sheet over her head.*

ROSIE. Whoo-oo-oo! I'm a ghost.

JACKIE. Oh – (*She drops the framed photo, which breaks.*) Look what you made me do!

ROSIE. Sorry.

MARGARET. What on earth are you doing Rosie? – Where's Mother?

ROSIE. We're folding sheets. The landing's a snow storm.

MARGARET (*weary*). Oh dear. I'd better go and look. – Jackie, you pick up the pieces. (*She exits.*)

ROSIE. Never mind Jackie. (*Kisses her.*) Look. Gran's cut holes for eyes in this sheet. She's done one for herself too, that'll give Mum a fright.

JACKIE (*laughs*). Oh Rosie . . .

ROSIE. What?

JACKIE. I don't know . . .

ROSIE. What's up?

JACKIE *fights tears. After a moment.*

JACKIE. Rosie, you must understand – (*Slight pause.*) Mummy has – a lot to cope with.

ROSIE. Oh, she's been telling you about Dad, hasn't she.

JACKIE. What about Dad?

ROSIE. Don't sound so worried. Why d'you always think things are your fault, Jackie?

JACKIE. – Does Mum work late?

ROSIE. Yeah. She's doing some new computer course in the evenings.

JACKIE. Does Dad mind?

ROSIE. Yeah, Mum drives him spare. They have rows a lot.

JACKIE (*anxious*). What about?

ROSIE. Oh I dunno, the washing or something. I just put my Walkman on.

JACKIE. Poor Mummy . . . why didn't she tell me about it?

ROSIE. Well she doesn't want you to know she's messed things up. – C'mon, help me rip this sheet.

JACKIE. What for?

They rip the sheet in half.

ROSIE. A banner. We're doing a Greenham protest outside the physics lab at school.

JACKIE. Why?

ROSIE. Secrecy kills. (*Pause.*) – Nuclear secrecy. (*Holds out half sheet.*) – Here, you can make one too.

JACKIE (*holds up sheet*). 'Sorry Mummy'.

ROSIE (*pause*). How old are you?

JACKIE. Thirty. Why?

ROSIE. You should stop that sort of thing now, or you never will. You should hear Mum's 'I'm sorry' voice on the phone to Gran.

JACKIE. Don't you worry about what Mummy thinks?

ROSIE. I worry about nuclear war, and not getting a job, and whether Mr Walsh the physics teacher fancies me. Mum doesn't understand.

JACKIE. Fancy not worrying.

ROSIE. He's old enough to be my Dad. Mega creepy. – You're old enough to be my Mum! (*Pause.*) I'm glad you're not.

JACKIE. Why?

ROSIE. Because it would be a mega-pain having to live up to you. Grandad used to go on and on about you, you know.

JACKIE. He disapproved of me.

ROSIE. He didn't.

JACKIE. I'm not how he thinks a woman should be.

ROSIE. That's what he liked! You are dumb.

JACKIE (*amazed*). It wasn't admiration you know, his will! It was revenge.

ROSIE. How?

JACKIE. I'd escaped. Families. – Nearly. He's made me responsible for all of you now.

ROSIE (*pause*). You are thick. He left you the money so you can open a gallery of your own.

JACKIE (*as she takes this in*). What would you do with the money Grandad left?

ROSIE. I'd buy a baseball jacket instead of this yucky anorak Mum makes me wear. I wouldn't give it all to Mum and Gran, like you. I'd give some to Green Peace. – C'mon, let's go in the garden and practise our banners.

ROSIE *opens the French windows and runs out swirling the sheet like a flag.* JACKIE *hesitates.* DORIS *enters, carrying a half-filled binliner.*

DORIS. There's some washing flapping in the garden.

JACKIE. It's Rosie. She wants to change the world. (*Pulls French windows shut.*)

DORIS. You used to be like that.

JACKIE. Have I changed so much?

DORIS (*watches* ROSIE). It was thick snow, that winter you came to stay. After Margaret had taken Rosie. – Not that you were in much of a state to enjoy Christmas.

JACKIE. You've still got my letter?

DORIS. Of course.

JACKIE. – Rosie must have it the day she's sixteen.

DORIS. Oh you make me so angry, Jackie! – You have to ask for what you want.

JACKIE. Granny, I can't!

DORIS. You can.

JACKIE. But Mummy's got so much to – it's not a good time for her.

DORIS. There's always an excuse. (*Pause.*) I never did ask for what I wanted. Resentment is a terrible thing, Jackie. You don't want to be resenting somebody at the end of your life.

JACKIE (*avoiding this*). What's in the binliner?

DORIS (*stiffly*). The pale blue curtains from the bedroom.

JACKIE. Oh good. Pale blue's your favourite, isn't it.

DORIS. Jack chose all the colours in this house (*Slight pause.*) Very artistic, visitors used to say. (*Pause.*) Scarlet, I'll have in my new house (*Pause.*)

Enter MARGARET carrying a binliner. As she puts it down.

MARGARET. Everything in the binliner is for Oxfam.

DORIS. Nothing ventured, Jackie.

JACKIE. Mummy . . .

MARGARET. Jackie, if you're not doing anything, there's the spare room to sort out.

JACKIE. Yes, Mummy.

There is a rumbling noise beyond the hall.

DORIS. I told you that boiler wasn't right, Margaret.

MARGARET. Yes Mother. (*She exits.*)

JACKIE (*picks up binliner with curtains which DORIS brought in*). Shall I put these curtains with the stuff for Oxfam, Granny?

DORIS. There's something else in that bag, Jackie. Some things you left with me once.

JACKIE. What?

DORIS. The babyclothes.

JACKIE (*pause – can't cope*). I'd better go and see if everything's all right in the kitchen.

DORIS. Are you going to give them away?

JACKIE. No. – Thank you, for keeping them safe, Granny.

JACKIE exits. DORIS opens the French windows.

DORIS. Rosie!

ROSIE comes in laughing and breathless, with the banner.

It's a waste of time. The world's going to end soon, I saw it on the television.

ROSIE. That's only the official view, you mustn't believe them . . . But it was scary when it blew up, wasn't it?

MARGARET (*entering*). What's blown up, Rosie dear?

ROSIE. The world.

MARGARET. Oh. That's all right. I thought it was something else.

DORIS. What?

MARGARET. Nothing, Mother.

DORIS. We thought perhaps the kitchen ceiling had come down. Jackie went to have a look. She's so good at that sort of thing.

MARGARET (*wearily*). Yes Mother. (*Exits.*)

DORIS. They work too hard.

ROSIE. You shouldn't wind them up.

DORIS. You should be helping them.

ROSIE. They'd only say I was more trouble.

They smile.

DORIS. I'll show you something. (*Pulls the dustsheet of the piano from Act One.*)

ROSIE (*pause*). It's the piano.

DORIS. Don't you like it?

ROSIE. We've got a synth at school.

DORIS. I had a friend called Cynth.

ROSIE. What's this? (*Picks up a plate on top of the piano.*)

DORIS. It's a salver. Jack's employees gave it him on his retirement. It's only plate, of course.

ROSIE(*sniffs*). The silver smells funny. I hate old things.

DORIS. You hate dead things, not old things, Rosie. (*Pause.*) So do I. (*Pause.*) I'm old.

ROSIE. Hold this. So you can see your face in it. (DORIS *holds the plate*.) Sit down on the piano stool. (DORIS *does so.*)

DORIS. What are you going to do?

ROSIE. Aha. Close you eyes.

ROSIE *stands behind her and puts her hands on* DORIS's *cheeks, gently pulling the skin back and taut.*)

ROSIE. Smooth the wrinkles away . . .

DORIS. Nice warm hands, Rosie.

ROSIE. Now open your eyes, Gran.

DORIS. Oh! (*She studies her reflection.*)

ROSIE. There, see. You're not old really. Only on the surface. (*A moment. Then* ROSIE *lets go.*) My outside's the same as my inside. That's why when I talk Mum thinks I'm being rude.

DORIS(*gets up, puts the salver in the box*). When you're old . . . if you're rude . . . they just think your mind is going. (*Pause.*) They never understand that it's anger. (*Pause.*) Help me polish the piano.

ROSIE. Do I have to?

DORIS. There's some dusters and polish in Margaret's holdall.

ROSIE. (*passes them. Reads tin*). 'Bradley's beeswax.' With a picture of a bee. Here.

DORIS. That's Jack's firm, of course. (*Tries, then.*) Can you unscrew it?

ROSIE (*does so*). What was your surname, Gran?

DORIS. Partington. Here, you take this cloth, and do the legs.

ROSIE *does.*

They polish the piano during the following.

ROSIE. We're doing a project about you at school.

DORIS. About me?

ROSIE. Yeah, you're working class Lancashire, aren't you?

DORIS. Do I look like it?

ROSIE. Yeah . . . (*As if from school book.*) 'Oldham families were all cotton or paper. Despite the decline in the manufacturing industries, community spirit remained strong.'

DORIS(*reminiscing*). You'd give a neighbour a bit of sugar, bit of soap, what they needed. When the King came, we scooped up the manure for the tomatoes. Pride costs nothing.

ROSIE. That's what they said on the documentary we saw at school.

DORIS. Did they now. You've missed a bit there, see. When Mother and I arrived in Jubilee Street, the landlady, a big woman, arms like beef, though she wore fancy hats, said 'I didn't know you had a babby'. 'You never asked', said Mother. She did! And that was that.

ROSIE. You didn't have a Dad?

DORIS. No.

ROSIE. Does Mum know?

DORIS. No.

ROSIE. Can it be our secret?

DORIS. If you like, Rosie. Of course people gossiped, but the girl next door was illegitimate too, it was more common than they put on those documentaries. I was instilled. To get on. Work hard and you will rise like bread, my mother said – Are you polishing that, or just resting your arm? – No one's ever told me what to do. Of course by the time I met Jack the neighbourhood wasn't what it used to be. Wicked things, even in Oldham. Well, there was the Depression. When you've got no job you lose a sense of things. But we worked. We moved up. To Cheadle Hulme! (*Pause.*) It was very – (*Pause.*) – snob. When Jack's parents came visiting I used to borrow the silver teapot from Next Door. Got in a fix one day, because Next Door's in-laws popped by the same afternoon. We had to pass it through the window, back and forth. (*Pause.*) I never used bicarb, for my scones, just elbow (*Rubs.*) There now. We can see our faces in it. (*Pause. Both admire it.*) It will fetch quite a bit, I fancy.

ROSIE. You can sell pianos through the small-ads.

DORIS. Jackie's organised an auction. hasn't she? Put these cloths away, they're soiled now.

ROSIE *opens* MARGARET's *binliner, thinking it's rubbish.*

DORIS. That's not rubbish –

ROSIE. Hey it's full of clothes! (*Tips the binliner all over the floor. Picks some up.*) Cheesecloth and flares! Yuck. I didn't know you were a hippy once, Gran.

DORIS. Oh quite a – what's the word – 'swinger'.

ROSIE. No kidding?

DORIS. No. (*Pause.*) Those were Jackie's – she came to stay with us once, left some things she didn't need any more.

ROSIE. Aren't they revolting! My big sister in these! (*Pulls out the ski pants* MARGARET *wore in Act One, Scene Seven.*) Oh, can I have these ski pants?

DORIS. You can have what you like. Margaret obviously doesn't care for any of them. Everything's throwaway now, of course.

ROSIE. But these are brill Gran! Mega trendy!

ROSIE *pulls ski pants over her tights and skirt.*

DORIS. You don't want those slacks. There's a nice beige skirt here, see love. (*Picks out skirt she wore in Act One, Scene Seven.*) Margaret bought those . . . 'Pants' . . . (*Disdain.*) They're American.

ROSIE. Are they real fifties?

DORIS. There's generations here, all mixed up, if you poke about. (*Rummages in binliner.*)

MARGARET *re-enters and goes to her holdall.*)

MARGARET. Don't say I didn't bring rubber gloves . . .

She pulls a pair from her holdall and puts them on during:

ROSIE. Mum, look! (*Silence.*) – D'you recognise them? (*Silence.*) Gee, ah simply must do mah nails! (ROSIE *parades about.*) – Mum?

MARGARET. Rosie we haven't time for dressing up games.

DORIS. I think they rather suit her, Margaret.

ROSIE. They're really sexy. I can't imagine you fitting into these, Mum! – Did she look nice in them, Gran?

Pause

MARGARET. Did I Mother?

Pause

ROSIE. Can't you remember that far back?

DORIS. You only remember what you want.

MARGARET. Rosie, clear up this mess. We're going as soon as Jackie's fixed the boiler. (*She exits.*)

ROSIE. I'm keeping these on for going home. Will you help me put my hair up, like they did?

DORIS (*helps* ROSIE *put her hair up*). A beehive? Sugar and water you need for that.

ROSIE (*delight*). – Like a punk!

They are stuffing clothes back into the binliner.

(*Amused.*) – Shall I keep this hippy stuff to show Jackie?

DORIS. I wouldn't bother.

ROSIE. Why not? – Really embarrass her!

DORIS. Not all memories are pleasant. (*Beat.*)

ROSIE. We should hide some clothes in the cellar, for someone to find in a hundred years . . .

DORIS *ties the binliner shut.* ROSIE *reaches for the other one.*

ROSIE. What's in here?

DORIS. – Oh, Just some old curtains.

ROSIE (*opens it*). What sweet little baby clothes! (*Tips them all over the floor.*) – You're not looking, Gran!

DORIS. Put those back in the bag, Rosie.

ROSIE. I want this one with the little rabbits on.

DORIS. No. That belongs to Jackie.

ROSIE. I'll ask Jackie then.

DORIS. I should have known . . .

Enter JACKIE, *distracted.*

JACKIE. Did I leave the stepladder in here?

She stops, seeing the babyclothes everywhere.

ROSIE (*holds up rabbit dress*). Look what I found!

JACKIE (*pause*). Not your rabbit dress.

ROSIE. – Mine? Gran, you said this was Jackie's.

DORIS. Did I? Well, you ask Jackie.

ROSIE *looks at* JACKIE

JACKIE (*slowly*). I bought it for you, Rosie.

MARGARET (*calls from the hall*). Jackie!

ROSIE *whips the rabbit dress behind her just as* MARGARET *enters on the line.*

MARGARET. Are you helping me or not?

She stops and takes in the scene.

ROSIE. Guess what Mum, you'll never guess!

MARGARET (*terror*). What.

ROSIE. GUESS!

She brings out the rabbit dress from behind her back.) – My baby dress! (*Pause.*) And guess what Jackie told me –

MARGARET (*giddy*). No . . .

JACKIE. It's okay everyone. Mummy it's okay.

She goes to MARGARET *but they can't hold each other.*

ROSIE. What?

JACKIE. Mummy's . . . not feeling well. Are you?

MARGARET. I'm perfectly all right!

Stasis.

DORIS. I think I've had enough for today.

JACKIE. Yes, it's getting late, isn't it.

ROSIE. It's half past five, you wallies!

MARGARET. Rosie, don't shout.

JACKIE. Mummy, are you all right?

DORIS. I expect she's been overdoing it.

MARGARET. Rosie put those babyclothes in the bag for Oxfam.

ROSIE. Oh Mum, don't be BORING.

JACKIE. Rosie! She's just sitting down.

ROSIE. I CAN SEE SHE'S SITTING DOWN!

DORIS. You're tired, dear.

ROSIE. I'm NOT TIRED!

JACKIE. You are!

ROSIE. Not you too!

DORIS. Margaret, have you seen my piano?

MARGARET. It's over there, Mother.

DORIS. I KNOW. I'm talking about the polish. You've not even noticed, have you?

MARGARET. Oh MOTHER! What did you do that for? It'll only need polishing again after the move.

DORIS. I'm selling it. At the auction.

MARGARET. But it's the only thing Father left for you.

DORIS. It was mine anyway. I bought it with my savings from teaching, when I got married. (*Pause.*) You never knew, did you?

MARGARET. You can't . . .

ROSIE. 'Course she can.

JACKIE. Food; everyone into the car.

ROSIE. I'm not hungry yet.

MARGARET. Mother needs to have her tea promptly, don't you dear?

DORIS. Oh I'm no trouble. I shall have a boiled egg.

ROSIE. Can we go to MacDonald's? Yeah!

JACKIE. We're all going to my flat.

MARGARET. You don't cook, Jackie.

JACKIE. We're getting a take-out Indian. There's a good place on the Stockport Road.

MARGARET. Mother can't possibly chew spare ribs.

DORIS. Chew what?

ROSIE. I hate curry. I want a MacDonalds. Can I keep these on?

DORIS. Yes.

MARGARET. No. Have you got your handbag, Mother?

DORIS. I don't need helping, thank you. Are you going home in rubber gloves?

JACKIE. Mummy, are you okay to drive, if I take the van?

MARGARET (*picks up thermos and thermos cup*). Does anyone want this tea . . .?

ROSIE. Mu-um, it's cold. – Knowing you, you'll probably take it home and save it for tomorrow.

MARGARET. Rosie! (*She tips tea into thermos and screws cup on.*)

JACKIE. I'll take these out to the van. (*Goes to the binliners. Sees a dress lying behind them.*) What's this dress? I didn't see it before – it looks like an original 1920s!

DORIS. I think there was a tea stain . . . no, it was a grass stain . . . I wore that frock the day that Jack proposed.

JACKIE. Do you want to keep it?

JACKIE *hesitates, holding up the dress. No response. She puts it in the binliner and ties it shut.*

MARGARET. I'm going to check the windows and turn the power off. You two get in the car. (*Exits.*)

JACKIE. I'll see you both back at my flat. (*Hesitates.*) Look at you with your hair up like that, Rosie! I wish you were still a baby. You were so sweet . . .

ROSIE. Was I?

DORIS. There was a time for babies, Jackie, and it's gone.

ROSIE. Ow, Jackie you always hug too hard!

DORIS. Truth will out, Jackie. Don't say I didn't warn you.

ROSIE. C'mon Gran, let's go.

JACKIE *looks at* DORIS, *picks up binliners and goes.*

DORIS. Come along Rosie, put your anorak on.

As DORIS *helps* ROSIE *into her anorak, the room is suddenly plunged into darkness.*

DORIS. Oh!

ROSIE. I left the big torch on the landing! – Wait there, Gran. (*Exits.*)

DORIS (*goes to French windows. Sound of wind*). Jack? Jack . . . You should see how the roses have all blown down in the garden . . . crushed . . . You rattle like a dry pod, now. Skin on your skull like frayed paper. (*Pause.*) I tried so hard, even in those last few years . . . Something nourishing and not difficult to chew . . . The tray pushed aside on your bed. You did that deliberately, didn't you? (*Pause.*) When you died and the nurses left me alone with you, to pray I suppose, I climbed into bed beside you, yes I did, lay beside you then . . . the sun was shining through the window, hot; only you were cold as ice.

ROSIE (*re-enters, carrying a round wooden board; also the flashlight, which she swings around the room until the beam comes to rest on* DORIS's *face.* DORIS *has been crying.*) – Gran? . . .

DORIS. Give me a minute. I'll put my hat and gloves on.

ROSIE. Gran? Hurry, what are you doing?

Car horn honks outside.

DORIS. Are they waiting for us?

ROSIE (*gently*). You haven't got any gloves . . . Oh Gran. (*Goes to* DORIS. *A split second of hesitation.*)

DORIS. Don't kiss –

ROSIE. Yes! (ROSIE *kisses* DORIS. DORIS *strokes* ROSIE's *hair.*)

DORIS. Lovely hair . . . mine are all old grey hairs . . .

ROSIE (*holds up a wooden board*). Look, Gran, look what I found in the spare room. What is it?

DORIS. Solitaire. Why, that was my mother's, she gave it me. It's a game. I used to sit and play it in the evenings, while Jack read the papers. You have to get rid of all the marbles from the holes in the board, until there is just one left, in the centre. Solitaire.

Car horn sounds again.

ROSIE. Can we take it with us?

DORIS. Yes, if you want, Rosie.

ROSIE. Will you show me how to do it?

DORIS. If you come and visit me. Put your hood up now, it's snowing out.

ROSIE *takes the Solitaire board and flashlight. She swings the beam round the room one last time. As they move to go, the sound of wind and snow increases.*

Blackout.

Interval.

ACT THREE

Scene One

The backyard of DORIS's *terrace house in Oldham, early April 1987.* DORIS *is 87, wears a floral overall;* MARGARET *is 56, dressed in the sensible suit she wears to work, wearing an apron she has borrowed from* DORIS. *They are chatting as they come out of the back kitchen door,* DORIS *guiding* MARGARET. MARGARET *carrying a tray of small geraniums in pots,* DORIS *carrying a kneeler. They kneel beside a tub and a bag of potting compost.*

DORIS. See dear, all those are from the one plant I brought with me from Cheadle Hulme.

MARGARET. I've had mine in the kitchen all winter, but they've not done so well.

DORIS. Oh you have to cut them right down until they're just dry sticks, then all of a sudden, it seems, they start producing new leaves.

MARGARET. They'll look lovely here.

DORIS. I've had a postcard from Rosie. She and Jackie seem to be having a lovely time.

MARGARET. Yes. It's very quiet at home.

Pause. MARGARET *continues planting a geranium in the tub.*

DORIS. You look thinner. Are you eating properly?

MARGARET. What do you mean?

DORIS. Don't crowd the roots – Well – you coming all the way from London like this – on a Tuesday!

MARGARET. Can't I even come and see you for the day without –

DORIS. Usually you're so busy, at that office . . . never have time to come and visit.

MARGARET. Yes well I took the day off!

DORIS. No need to snap dear.

Pause. MARGARET *digs a hole.*

MARGARET. You've transformed this backyard, I must say. The trellis is nice.

DORIS. Yes, I'm quite proud, it's only five years since the move. Cheadle Hulme will be a mass of blossom, now, of course. The jasmine hasn't done very well, but then it's been such a Spring.

MARGARET. Good. (*Pause.*) I mean, sorry, yes. – It's been awful, Spring, hasn't it.

DORIS. How are your geranium tubs doing?

MARGARET. Mmm.

DORIS. I ate my shoe this afternoon.

MARGARET. Yes. (*Picks a leaf, stares at it.*)

DORIS. Margaret, you're not listening to a word I'm saying, are you?

MARGARET. Of course . . .

DORIS. What's wrong, Margaret?

MARGARET. What do you mean, what's wrong?

DORIS. You're upset.

MARGARET. I'm probably upset because you're accusing me of being upset.

DORIS (*smoothly*). I'm not accusing you. Don't take umbrage.

MARGARET. Really Mother. I make the effort to come here for a friendly visit and you react as though there's something wrong! Can't I even have a normal conversation with my own Mother?

DORIS. I don't know, dear.

MARGARET. What do you mean, you don't know? (*Pause.*) And don't call me 'dear'!

DORIS. Trains from London are so expensive at this time of day.

MARGARET. There, see? We can't even talk without the housekeeping coming into it.

DORIS (*pause. Gently*). What is it dear? It's Ken, isn't it (*Silence.*) . . . He's not been made redundant? (*Silence.*)

MARGARET (*pause*). I don't know.

DORIS. What do you mean, you don't know.

MARGARET. I haven't seen Ken for a week, Mother. (*Pause.*) I don't think it's another woman. He's not like that. And we've always been very happy. I know it happens to one in three marriages these days, but – you don't think of yourself as a statistic, do you? (*Pause.*) Mummy, I still want him.

DORIS. Your Father . . . stopped 'wanting me', many years ago. One didn't divorce, then. I thought if I persisted in loving him . . . I wanted to – to be desired. (*Pause.*) The night before he died, we embraced. He held my hand; he said that he loved me most that night. I believed him . . . Was it worth it, I ask myself? (*Silence.*) You've made more of your life. A job and that.

MARGARET. Exactly. It's all my fault. He loved me, Mother . . . but he didn't want to share me.

DORIS. With who?

MARGARET. With the job. Trying to work and look after Rosie . . . Well I had to work, London's so expensive now. (*Pause.*) But Ken married a wife, not a working mother.

DORIS. You expected too much. So did I. And Jackie expects even more. (*Pause.*) My father turned up once, after we'd moved to Jubilee Street. Mother took him back, of course. I saw the marks, when she was bathing in front of the fire. She said it was because he loved her so much, he hugged her too tight. (*Pause.*) When I think about Jack, I think, well, I was lucky really.

DORIS *gently lowers the geranium plant into the hole* MARGARET *has dug.* MARGARET *pats soil around it.*

DORIS. Come in the cottage with me, dear. There's something I want to give you. (*Pause.*) You've never seen a photograph of my Mother, have you?

MARGARET (*a white lie*). No.

MARGARET *stands and helps* DORIS *stand.* DORIS *takes* MARGARET *by the arm as they go in.*

Scene Two

Croydon, London, early April 1987, four days later. A bright sunny morning in MARGARET'*s office, but traffic noise outside. A desk, a telephone, a typewriter, a pot of geraniums and a photo frame.* MARGARET *is 56,* JACKIE *is 34,* ROSIE *is 15 and a half.*

MARGARET *is seated, uncovering the typewriter. She wears a sensible suit as in the previous scene.*

ROSIE (*enters with an orange kite and a bundle of letters, which she puts on* MARGARET's *desk. She wears colourful and trendy holiday clothes.*) Morning post, Mrs Metcalfe.

MARGARET. Rosie! What on earth are you doing here?

ROSIE (*kisses* MARGARET. *Makes the kite swoop round the office space*). Look! Isn't it beautiful!

MARGARET. Have you been home yet?

ROSIE. No. We came straight from Gatwick, all the way in a taxi, can you imagine! But Jackie says when it's important you have to do these things.

MARGARET (*touching her hair.*) Is she here too?

ROSIE. Yes. Only she's gone in the third floor Ladies to change into her Art Dealer dress. She doesn't want you to see her looking a mess.

MARGARET. Is she going straight back to work?

ROSIE. There's some meeting about the future of her gallery, with the Manchester City Council. (*She swoops the kite.*)

MARGARET. But you've both been travelling all night!

ROSIE. So?

MARGARET. You'd better get that out of sight before Mr Reece arrives at nine.

ROSIE. Don't you like it? Such style, the Italians.

MARGARET. How was Venice?

ROSIE. Brilliant! 'Fettucine alla casa, va bene?'! The food was marvellous. Dad would have hated it!

MARGARET. I'm sure.

ROSIE. I can't believe it's only two weeks! What have you been up to? You didn't clean my room?

MARGARET. I went to visit Granny.

ROSIE. I sent her a postcard of the beach where we flew this kite. Also we brought some Chianti back for Dad, and you'll never guess what we've brought you! Did Dad water my tomatoes?

MARGARET. (*pause*). Dad's gone away for the week. What did you like best in Venice?

ROSIE. Oh, definitely the carnival. We stayed up all night, everyone wore masks like birds, that's when I saw the kites. We had breakfast at San Marco's, and this man fell in love with Jackie, so I just stared into the canal and ordered another cappucino, and pretended I was waiting for a gondola. And then it turned out it was me he fancied, and Jackie got very cross with him in Italian, and we had to leave.

MARGARET. I hope you didn't stay up every night?

ROSIE. Oh yes – Mum, of course not. I mean – Jackie's so sweet, she was trying so hard to be like you.

MARGARET. Like me?

ROSIE. Yes. I can't think of anyone less like a mother! (*Pause.*) You know Mum, sometimes you have to be a bit silly with Jackie just to get her to relax. She needs . . .

MARGARET. What does she need?

ROSIE. . . . I don't know . . . it's hard to explain. (*Thinks.*) She's so restless: she's always looking for something to do. We spent a whole day trekking round museums but she could never find the picture she wanted. After I'd got this kite, we went to this incredible long beach, ran for miles. (*Swoops kite.*) We were shouting because of the wind, and Jackie got the kite to do a perfect circle in the sky . . . Oh Mum, it was such a brilliant day . . . Will you stop opening letters for a minute –

MARGARET. I'm at work.

ROSIE. Yes, but I have to tell you something! Oh Mum, it's incredible!

MARGARET. What dear?

ROSIE. Well, I asked Jackie – I couldn't believe she'd agree – I want to go and live with her in Manchester!

MARGARET (*long pause*). What about your exams?

ROSIE. Oh, I won't go till the summer, of course. Anyway, Jackie says we have to discuss it with you and Dad first. (*Pause.*) Mum . . .?

MARGARET. You've no idea. Jackie can't cook, she'll forget to wash your clothes . . .

ROSIE. I know! She's so useless at most things. Not like you. (*Pause.*) She needs me. (*Pause.*) I'll come back and visit, lots.

MARGARET. Whenever you can afford the fare.

ROSIE. Oh Jackie will pay. She says we'll both visit. She comes to London all the time, anyway.

MARGARET. Does she?

ROSIE (*cuts in*). You said! Don't you remember? You promised, after my exams I could do whatever I wanted.

MARGARET (*long pause*). Yes, I did. (*Turns away, afraid she's going to cry.*) I've got to . . . write a letter, Rosie, can you wait outside a minute . . .

ROSIE *exits, swooping the kite as she goes.* JACKIE *and* ROSIE *meet in the corridor.* JACKIE *is wearing a flowery dress, carrying a Chinese lacquered briefcase and a blue kite.*

ROSIE. Don't go in. (*Surveys* JACKIE.) You've spoiled it now, Miss Executive. You should go to work wearing that turquoise thing.

JACKIE. That was a beach dress.

ROSIE. Suited you much better.

JACKIE. It's an incredibly important meeting.

ROSIE. All the more reason to let them see what you're really like.

JACKIE. I can't start now.

ROSIE. You could. If you really wanted. Come outside and fly this kite with me.

JACKIE. I want to see Mummy.

ROSIE. She's busy.

JACKIE. I'll sit in her office and prepare for my meeting.

ROSIE. See – now you're being all business woman again!

JACKIE. Calm down. You're not at home now.

ROSIE. Mum isn't like you when she's at work. (*Goes, swooping the kite.*)

JACKIE (*enters the office*). Mummy! I'm sorry. Didn't you get the message? The delay was twelve hours in the end, airport like an oven.

MARGARET. Rosie's hopelessly over-excited.

JACKIE. I know mummy, I couldn't get her to sleep. But she's been so good all holiday, you don't need to worry. She's very sensible for fifteen. Wouldn't let me swim too far out.

MARGARET. She'll be tired for the first day of term now.

JACKIE. That's three days away!

MARGARET. There's all her clothes to wash.

JACKIE. I'd do it, but I've . . .

MARGARET. Got to go back to Manchester for a meeting.

JACKIE (*pause*). Rosie can wash her own things. She did all our clothes one evening, fixed up a line on the balcony.

MARGARET. It's an adventure with you. (*Pause.*) You should see her bedroom, it's like a junkyard – clothes, glue, paint.

JACKIE. She's very creative. Kept writing poetry in the restaurant.

MARGARET. She's full of crazy ideas. (*Testing* JACKIE.)

JACKIE (*pause. Cautious*). Is she? (*No reply from* MARGARET.) It's just her energy, isn't it.

MARGARET. Well of course with you . . .

JACKIE. She talks about you a lot.

MARGARET. What about?

JACKIE. Oh, I only mean your job. She wanted to show me all round where you work.

MARGARET. Did she?

JACKIE. You didn't tell me you were promoted last year. (*Looks over* MARGARET's *shoulder at the letters she is opening.*)

MARGARET. It's nothing glamorous.

JACKIE. You know I'd be useless at this. My typing's awful . . . Do you have to reply to all these?

MARGARET. Mr Reece dictates, I spend the rest of the morning unravelling his grammar, otherwise British Microwaves would never have any export trade. These young graduates.

JACKIE. I hope they pay you the right scale. You're the one who does all the work.

MARGARET. I'm only his personal assistant.

JACKIE. Don't say 'only'.

MARGARET. Oh I was lucky. My typing speeds are very ordinary. It's only that I've got Pitman's Classic and most of the girls don't learn shorthand these days.

JACKIE. I'm sure it's other qualities got you this job, Mummy.

MARGARET (*pause. Pleased*). It's funny, hearing 'Mummy' in this place. You do a job, people treat you differently.

JACKIE. It's only how you treat yourself.

MARGARET (*pause*). You look radiant dear.

JACKIE. Swimming and sea air. (*Quiet.*) Bit of sun, Mummy. Do you good, too.

MARGARET (*quiet*). Sat in the garden this weekend. Been very . . . Been a relief, you having Rosie for these two weeks.

JACKIE (*pause*). I hope you kept the appointment? She's a nice woman, isn't she?

MARGARET. It was a very expensive looking waiting room.

JACKIE. Mummy, I asked you to see the specialist, not the wallpaper. What did she say?

MARGARET. Oh – Nothing much.

JACKIE. Did she do some tests?

MARGARET. No.

JACKIE. No?

MARGARET. Says I'm fine. Just menopause, probably.

JACKIE (*pause*). Honestly?

MARGARET (*pause*).What do you mean?

JACKIE. Well – (*Pause.*) – That's such a relief! (*Laughs.*) Oh Mummy. We even got a taxi all the way here!

MARGARET (*pause*). Now you can go and catch your train to Manchester, can't you.

JACKIE. Mum . . . May Bank holiday, come and stay with me. Just you, and we'll . . .

MARGARET. Fly kites.

JACKIE (*gives her the blue kite*). Oh yes, Rosie and I bought you a kite. She says Daddy will show you how to fly it, but I said you're an expert. Do you remember, how you took me flying kites in Richmond Park, and once it got stuck in a chestnut tree, and all the conkers came down?

MARGARET. I thought you'd wiped out that little girl.

JACKIE. So did I. Rosie won't. She'll have kites in her office, or whatever. (*Pause.*) I used to wear suits, when I first started my job. (*Bends and picks up a photo frame.*) Is this Cornwall? . . . Oh can I have a copy? Doesn't Rosie look sweet!

MARGARET (*pause*). Rosie's told me, Jackie.

JACKIE (*terrified*). I wasn't going to –

MARGARET. No, I expect you had another date planned when you were going to tell me that you'd like Rosie back. Or perhaps you were just going to tell me over the phone.

JACKIE. . . . You need time, to decide . . . in the summer –

MARGARET. It's not my decision. It's Rosie's. And she's made her mind up. (*Pause.*) I knew she'd say it one day. Like one of those fairytales.

JACKIE. You haven't told her!

MARGARET. Of course not. She still thinks you're big sister, that's why it's so magical to her.

JACKIE. We were running along this dazzling beach. I thought, is that what I've missed?

MARGARET. Years and years and years you've lost, Jackie. Birthdays and first snowman and learning to ride a bicycle and new front teeth. You can't pull them back.

JACKIE. I can make up for it – somehow –

MARGARET. You can't. Those are my years.

JACKIE. She must remember – I visited!

MARGARET. Treats, she's had with you. A day here and there. That never fooled her. But I let it fool you. I'm the woman who sat up all night with the sick child, who didn't mind all her best crockery getting broken over the years.

JACKIE. Mummy . . .

MARGARET(*long pause. Cool*). What time's your train?

JACKIE. 9.45 – no – I could get the 10.45.

MARGARET. You mustn't miss your meeting.

JACKIE. It would give us another hour. I wish we weren't in your office! (*Panics.*) Where's Rosie gone?

MARGARET. Are you going to catch that train, or stay here? You can't do both.

Pause. JACKIE *agonises.*

MARGARET. I'll phone you a taxi. (MARGARET *dials, waits, the line is engaged.*)

JACKIE (*quietly*). You know Mummy, the Gallery and everything, I couldn't have done it without you. You can't be a mother and then cancel Christmas to be in New York.

MARGARET (*telephone connects*). Taxi to East Croydon station please, immediately. British Microwaves, front entrance. (*Puts receiver down.*)

JACKIE. Come and stay, show me how you do things, how Rosie would like her room decorated.

MARGARET. No Jackie, I shall just put a label around Rosie's neck, and send her Red Star. (*Doesn't look at* JACKIE *any more, busies herself with papers.*) It's gone nine. I wonder where Mr Reece is?

JACKIE *runs out of the room.*

MARGARET (*bursts into tears. Telephone rings*). Hello? Hello. Yes, I'll be with you directly. (*Puts down the receiver.*) Oh God, my mascara – all over the letters.(*Picks up notebook to go.*) It will be strange. I'm a single woman again. (*Calms herself.*) I'll oversleep. (*Hesitates then dials telephone.*) Hello? Manchester City Art Gallery? Yes, I'd like to leave a message for Jackie Metcalfe. Just say – (*Pause.*) – May Bank Holiday will be fine. (*Puts phone down and walks out of the office. Blackout.*)

Scene Three

The Wasteland. Cats wail. Almost dark. We see the glint of faces and hands.

JACKIE. Harelip and eye of bat.

ROSIE. Poisoned dewdrop and tail of cat.

JACKIE. Put it in a monkey's hat.

DORIS. What's a monkey's hat?

JACKIE. Sssh!

ROSIE. You can't have harelip.

JACKIE. Sssh!

DORIS. Why?

ROSIE. It's something real. You get it. I've seen a lady with it in the opticians.

DORIS. What's it like?

JACKIE. Sssh! I can't con-centrate. This is a laboratory. (*Stirring twig potage.*)

ROSIE. It's a sort of slit in your mouth, goes up your nose.

DORIS. Eugh.

ROSIE. You're born with it. It means you're missing a bit in the head, too.

JACKIE. Shut up!

DORIS. Let's go and have a look!

ROSIE. Optician's closed.

JACKIE (*mysteriously*). She didn't used to have it. It grew.

ROSIE. Honest?

JACKIE. Maybe *we* did it. (*Pause.*)

ROSIE. How could we . . .

DORIS. Could we?

JACKIE *(grand)* I can tell you what her name is.

ROSIE. Go on.

JACKIE. Mrs Worsley.

DORIS. That's right!

JACKIE. See? Proves it. Our powers.

DORIS. What powers?

JACKIE. In the earth.

ROSIE. What happens to people when they die, then?

JACKIE. They rot. Worms go in their nose and out their eyeballs.

DORIS. No! *(Starts to cry.)* I don't want to do that –

JACKIE. It's too late.

ROSIE. I don't want to do that to Mum!

JACKIE. 'S too late. Was her idea.

DORIS. No!

ROSIE. No it wasn't, it was yours.

DORIS. Stop it!

ROSIE. Stop the spell.

DORIS. Make it go backwards!

JACKIE. You can't make someone's life go backwards.

ROSIE. I'm going to tell her – c'mon! *(Grabs* DORIS *and they run off.)*

DORIS. Wasn't me!

JACKIE. She'll be dead when you get there.

Cats wail. The shadowy figure of MARGARET *appears upstage.*

JACKIE. I didn't mean to do it! Don't leave me all alone!

She runs off.

Scene Four

MARGARET *in a hospital gown, with her hair scraped back. Her face is drawn, and very white. Late May 1987. Under anaesthetic. She has become only a voice.*

MARGARET. I know the door is here somewhere, if only I could find it, the door to the garden . . . Here's a door . . . the bathroom! . . . What a cold wind blowing through here . . . Why, here we are, on its iron legs, the white enamel bath . . . cold on your bare flesh, even in summer . . . goosepimples . . . Father's made his fortune! But we still have to save hot water . . . Everything is a sacrifice in this house. Everything – is – sacrificed for . . . Piano Tuition. Tu-ition . . . BUT! *(Whispers, conspiratorial.)* One must go to the bathroom and lock the door if one wants – needs – to CRY! . . . When you pull the plug out, the water gets sucked down with a roar . . . So they know I'm here . . . no privacy in this huge house . . . My parents are called, My parents are called . . . Guilt, and Duty . . . When *I* have babies, they will be called Sugar and Spice and all things nice . . . I will give them everything they want, and they will love me *(Pause.)* . . . Mother? . . . Mummy . . . What happens when you die? . . . I wish they wouldn't keep opening the door, it's so cold . . . I'm sure I can find the garden, if I just keep going.

Lights fade on her. We hear a baby crying, then a child crying. Fade out.

Scene Five

The garden of KEN *and* MARGARET's *suburban semi in Rayne's Park, London, late May 1987, early morning, 2 hours after Scene Four.* ROSIE *sits on the swing beneath the cherry tree with the old red tranny wearing one of* KEN's *jumpers, which is much too big, and jeans.* JACKIE *runs across the garden, hot and grubby, carrying her lacquered briefcase, dressed for work. Both have been up all night.*

LBC RADIO. More congestion on the North Circular, meanwhile the overturned tanker is still blocking the Blackwall Tunnel. And it's coming up to 8 o'clock, a lovely May morning . . . Looking down the Euston Road, here's to the girl in that blue Mini, a thought from the Beatles . . .(*Plays 'All You Need Is Love'.*)

JACKIE. Rosie? . . .

Silence. Hold this for as long as possible while JACKIE *has to cope with it.*

ROSIE. I hope you're a success, Jackie. A big, big success.

JACKIE. Rosie are you all right? Where's Daddy?

ROSIE. I hope lots of people came to your opening and thought your gallery was brill.

JACKIE. It was only twelve hours – I'd never have gone back to Manchester if I'd thought – after Daddy phoned last night, there were no more planes, I got the first plane I could this morning. If only . . .

ROSIE. In case you want to know, she died at 6.20 last night. Dad was with her. They said it was quicker at the end. It wasn't just stomach cancer, there were secondaries.

JACKIE (*goes to hug* ROSIE *who won't let her.*) If only I'd been here with you . . .

ROSIE (*turns away*). Did you sell lots of your paintings?

JACKIE. Rosie –

ROSIE. Did you?

JACKIE. I didn't sell any. I cancelled the opening.

ROSIE. I don't believe you. You'd never do that.

Silence.

JACKIE. What do we do . . . now? . . . I'll call a taxi to the hospital – do we have to take things – her birth certificate? . . . I don't know . . .

ROSIE. Dad's done all that. He's been brilliant, like it was before they split up. He knew where Mum kept the box that's got all the family stuff in it. Look – he said I could have this one – (*Holds out a photo.*) That's Mum holding me by the front door when I'd just arrived . . . And . . . (*Lays them on grass.*) – Here's Mum's birth certificate, . . . and here's mine.

Silence.

JACKIE. No.

ROSIE. So now I know.

JACKIE (*desperate*). I was going to tell you – in five months – when you were sixteen . . . Mummy said to wait till after your exams, so as not to upset you . . .

ROSIE (*has a handful of photos, throws them down one by one, except for one which she slips in her pocket*). 1972, my first birthday, 1973, my second birthday, Christmas 1975, 1976; then you were in South America, 1979 with the birthday cake, 1982 when we cleared Gran and Grandad's house, – and our holiday in Venice. (*Pause.*) Have them. Have them all.

JACKIE. Rosie – we've got to help each other now.

ROSIE. Why don't you go and get drunk, or whatever it is you lot do to show you're feeling something.

JACKIE. I wanted you to have opportunities I couldn't ever have given you.

ROSIE. No you didn't. You wanted your own life more than you wanted mine!

JACKIE. Don't!

ROSIE. If you were really my Mum you wouldn't have been able to give me away!

JACKIE. How dare you! (*Goes to hit* ROSIE *but cannot.*) You're at the centre of everything I do! (*Slight pause.*) Mummy treated me as though I'd simply fallen over and cut my knee, – picked me up and said you'll be all right now, it won't show much. She wanted to make it all better. (*Quiet.*) . . . She was the one who wanted it kept secret . . . I WANTED you, Rosie. (*Angry.*) For the first time in my life I took care of myself – refused joints, did exercises, went to the clinic. (*Pause.*) 'It's a girl'. (*Smiles irresistibly.*) – After you'd gone I tried to lose that memory. (*Pause. Effort.*) Graham . . . your Father. (*Silence.*) He couldn't be there the day you were born, he had to be in Liverpool. He was married. (*Emphatic.*) He loved me, he loved you, you must believe that! (*Pause.*) He said he'd leave his wife, but I knew he wouldn't; there were two children, the youngest was only four . . . we'd agreed, separate lives, I wanted to bring you up. He sent money. (*Pause.*) I took you to Lyme Park one day, I saw them together, across the lake, he was buying them ice creams, his wife was taking a photo. I think they live in Leeds now, I saw his name in the Guardian last year, an article about his photographs . . . (*Pause.*) It was a very cold winter after you were born. There were power cuts. I couldn't keep the room warm; there were no lights in the tower blocks; I knew he had an open fire, it was trendy; so we took a bus to Didsbury, big gardens, pine kitchens, made a change from concrete. I rang the bell. (*Stops.*) A Punjabi man answered, said he was sorry . . . they'd moved. By the time we got back to Mosside it was dark, the lift wasn't working – (*Stops.*) That was the night I phoned Mummy. (*Difficult.*) Asked her. (*Pause.*) I tried! I couldn't do it, Rosie. (*Pause.*) It doesn't matter how much you succeed afterwards, if you've failed once. (*Pause.*) After you'd gone . . . I kept waking in the night to feed you . . . A week . . . in the flat . . . Then I went back to art school. Sandra and Hugh thought I was inhuman. I remember the books that came out that winter – how to succeed as a single working mother – fairytales! (*Pause.*) Sandra and Hugh have a family now. Quite a few of my friends do. (*Pause.*) I could give you everything now. Rosie? . . .

ROSIE (*pause*). I used to hate you, only I never knew why. (*Gestures.*) Sit down on the swing. I'm going to Oldham, to live with Gran – Great-Gran. Dad says I can.

JACKIE *hesitates*). I'm frightened.

ROSIE (*gestures*). Sit down on the swing. Put your head back and look up through the cherry tree. The sky is falling. Mum used to sit here with me in her arms, and I'd pretend I was asleep. (*Gets up.*) I'm never having any children. (*Starts towards the house.*)

JACKIE. You might.

ROSIE *hears, but keeps walking away.*

JACKIE *goes to the swing.*

Lights fade to blackout.

Scene Six

The Wasteground, Oldham.
MARGARET *walks in, balancing on cracks of paving.*

MARGARET. King of the Golden River! (*Demonstrates invisible line.*) I'm the King.

JACKIE (*runs in*) Farmer Farmer, may I cross your golden river, just to take our Daddy's dinner.

JACKIE *runs to cross the line*, MARGARET *chases and catches her.*

MARGARET. You've got to do a dare . . . !

JACKIE. I've been in the boys' den . . .

MARGARET. And?

JACKIE. They wanted me to kill you.

MARGARET. It didn't work.

JACKIE. Sure?

MARGARET. Yes.

Slight pause.

JACKIE. The others won't play with me any more.

MARGARET. Tell you what.

JACKIE. What?

MARGARET. You can come with me. To my secret, secret hide.

MARGARET *holds out her hand.* MARGARET *and* JACKIE *run off together.*

Scene Seven

Oldham, September 1987. The backyard of DORIS's *end terrace cottage. Distant sound of children. Two deck chairs. Piano stool from Act One, on it the Solitaire board from Act Two. A tub of geraniums. A green kite.* ROSIE *is sunbathing in shorts and painted tee shirt, both of which she has tie-dyed herself, and she is wearing Walkman headphones, oblivious of all other noise. She hums 'Holding Back The Years', as she concentrates on the Solitaire game.*

DORIS (*appears upstage, holding up kite tail. Calls*). Is this right?

ROSIE (*hums*). . . . Holding back the years . . .

DORIS (*comes nearer*). Rosie? CAN YOU HEAR ME DEAR? (*Taps* ROSIE *on the shoulder.*)

ROSIE. SORRY! (*Removes headphones.*)

DORIS. You're shouting again, dear. Neighbours will think I'm deaf. (*Holds up kite tail.*) Is this right?

ROSIE. Looks great! Thanks. (*Picks up the kite.*) Here, just tie it on the bottom.

DORIS (*ties the kite tail to the kite*). Needs a stitch in it . . .

ROSIE (*holds the kite aloft*). What d'you think?

DORIS (*pause*). I preferred the blue ones.

ROSIE. Well they've ordered fifty, so I'm not complaining. (*Puts the kite down.*) Did ten this morning.

DORIS. I gathered that, from the state of the box room. Bits of string . . .

ROSIE. It's not for you to clear up. Sit down Doris, enjoy the sun.

DORIS (*sits*). I fancy one of those garden tables . . . white ones, with an umbrella. But they do cost, don't they?

ROSIE (*firmly*). When I've sold the next batch, maybe. We mustn't spend before we've paid off the overheads.

DORIS. You shouldn't be bothering your head with work on your birthday. (*Pause.*) Just like your mother.

ROSIE. Did you see her present!

DORIS. Mrs W saw me take it in. Postman couldn't get it through the letterbox.

ROSIE. It's one of her paintings.

DORIS. I propped it on the mantelpiece.

ROSIE. What d'you think.

DORIS (*pause*). I liked the gold frame. Looks expensive.

ROSIE. Gran! She did it specially for me.

   A lull. ROSIE *returns to Solitaire.*

ROSIE. You promised to show me how to solve the Solitaire, today.

DORIS. You work it out. (*She watches* ROSIE *for a moment.*) No cheating, mind. Took my Mother years to work it out. She showed me, but she made me vow never to tell anyone. I didn't even tell Jack, and husbands and wives aren't suppose to have any secrets, are they?

ROSIE. Listen, I've been trying all week, and I can't do it.

DORIS. One week is nothing.

   ROSIE *studies the board.*

   Isn't this sunshine cheering? (*She puts on a pair of mirrored sunglasses.*)

ROSIE. What do you think my next move should be?

DORIS. What do you think, Rosie?

ROSIE (*laughs*). Oh Doris, take my shades off!

DORIS. They're mine. Bought them at the checkout when I went for the ice cream.

ROSIE. There's a new Pakistani shop opened. Even cheaper than Kwiksave.

DORIS. Jack came home one night and I was sat in the dark. I told him, I'm economising. He said, that's just as well, you left the hall light on. (*Pause.*) You can't win.

ROSIE. You can. Look, double jump! Is that allowed?

DORIS. Yes. Do you know, I think I'll even take my stockings off, and then my legs can brown. (*Modestly reaches under her skirt and unhooks her stockings.*) Well, I may be as old as the Queen Mother, but *I* buy all my smalls in Top Shop.

ROSIE. Hmmm . . . (*Removes another marble.*)

DORIS. Do you know Rosie, there's no such snob as the snob who rises from the gutter . . .

ROSIE. Are you 'casting aspersions' again? Grubbing at the Royal Family this time, are you?

DORIS. No. As a matter of fact I was making an inference to my late husband. Jack would never have tolerated this lack of modesty in a woman. (*Pause.*) Although while we're on the subject, it is true that the Queen Mother was a Commoner before she married up.

ROSIE. AH! Triple jump! Fucking brill!

DORIS. Does one have to lower the tone of the afternoon quite so crudely?

ROSIE. Stop attempting posh, Doris. Your slip is showing.

DORIS. Is it? . . . Still, I don't suppose the Queen Mother does all her own washing . . . (*Leans back and closes her eyes.*)

ROSIE *puts headphones back on. Hums.*

A lull.

DORIS. I suppose now you've got hold of that game, I won't be hearing from you till the Christmas after next.

ROSIE (*singing softly. Moves a marble*). Ah!

DORIS (*opens her eyes*). What with that electronic earmuff you wear, night and day.

ROSIE (*studying the board*). Hmm . . .

DORIS. In my day, families practised the art of conversation

ROSIE. Aah! (*Removes another marble.*)

DORIS (*watches* ROSIE *fondly*). Your mother couldn't solve that. Though she tried.

ROSIE (*removes headphones*). Are you talking to me? (*Stretches.*) Mmm! It's hot, like being inside a blue balloon. (*Gazes out.*) The moors are clear today. We should've walked up to the Waterloo Memorial.

DORIS (*gazes out*). Wicked, sticking these tower blocks in the view.

ROSIE. It's so lovely here, Doris. (*Pause.*) Ken phoned to say happy birthday. I asked him to put some flowers on Margaret's grave today.

DORIS (*pause*). To think, Jack and I in this same street, 60 years ago – scrimping and saving so that our child would have a better start in life . . . You do what you believe is best for your daughter, you know Rosie, and then you find it wasn't what she wanted. Or needed.

ROSIE. Remember what Jackie said afterwards. We mustn't live in the past.

DORIS. Well I don't see that I've much of a future. Stuck here with my great-granddaughter in a two-up, two-down.

ROSIE. Gran!

DORIS (*winding her up*). Forced to do piecework, tying scraps of coloured paper to lengths of string all day long . . .

ROSIE. How much do you want that garden table . . . ?

DORIS. You fancy you can bribe your great-grandmother?

ROSIE. Yes.

DORIS (*pause*). How many did you say you wanted?

ROSIE. Fifty. By the end of the week. We can do them sitting out here.

DORIS. 'Campaign Kites' . . . Who'd have thought you'd earn a living off them. (ROSIE *moves another marble.*) Who are they for this time?

ROSIE. Green Peace.

DORIS. Had another phone call from that Animal Liberation man.

ROSIE. I won't do business with organizations that use violence. (*Pause.*) What did you tell him?

DORIS. That he was politically unsound.

ROSIE. That's a good phrase.

DORIS. Heard a girl say it at the evening class.

ROSIE. Let me guess . . . Tricia?

DORIS. No – a new girl in Women's Literature – She's from the tower block over there. I've met her in the Welfare with her two babbies, and do you know, she doesn't look the sort to even open a book. But she's quite the best, the comments she comes out with in class. She can't spell, of course. (*Pause.*) But it just goes to show: you can't judge by appearances. Jack was wrong. (*Pause.*) Even so, I do wish you wouldn't wear those dirty rags. You look . . . like a victim.

ROSIE. I made this tee-shirt. It got ripped at the last march. Perhaps someone will find it in our cellar one day, and remember. (*Pause.*) And remember me.

DORIS. At least you're not wounded inside.

Pause

ROSIE (*removes another marble*). . . . Look, this is a magic marble: when you hold it up to the sun there's a frozen fountain inside.

DORIS. It seems no time since you were trying to push that up your nose. (*Pause.*) I'm going to put our tea on. Can you pass my shoes?

ROSIE. I'll do it.

DORIS. No, it really is my turn.

ROSIE. – Have you got me a birthday cake!

DORIS. Yes.

ROSIE. I love you, Doris.

DORIS. A long time since anyone's said that to me. (*Pause.*) Sixty-one years, Jack and I were married. I don't think we liked each other very much. (*Pause.*) There's a letter here for you.

ROSIE. There's no address on it.

DORIS. It's from your mother. I've kept it safe in my scrapbox, with Jack's letters, and Margaret's exercise book, and the drawings Jackie did when she was a little girl. (*Pause.*) After Margaret took you to London, Jackie came to see me. Left some baby clothes, and asked me to give you this letter when you reached sixteen. Happy Birthday. (*Kisses* ROSIE. *Goes in to the cottage.*)

ROSIE *picks up the letter, opens it and reads.*

ROSIE. ' . . .I don't know if you'll ever love me as much as I love you. But one day you'll understand why I've done this to you, probably not until you are on your own yourself . . . ' (ROSIE *throws the letter down. After a moment she retrieves it. She concentrates on the Solitaire board and completes the game with a few last moves, so that one marble is left in the centre hole.*) Solitaire! (*Calls.*) Gran! Gran, guess what, I've discovered the secret, all by myself! Gran? I'll prove it to you, come and watch, I'm going to do it all over again now, so that I remember it always. You there Gran? (*Silence.*) Oh never mind.

ROSIE *puts the headphones back on and hums quietly. As she replaces all the marbles on the board,* JACKIE *appears upstage, dressed as in Act Three, Scene Five.* MARGARET *appears also, dressed as in Act Three, Scene Two. The blue kite flies up high over* MARGARET.

Scene Eight

Enter DORIS *in the 1920's print dress which* JACKIE *pulled from the box in Act Two and a straw hat trimmed with flowers. She is breathless and her hair is awry. It is May 1923.*

DORIS. Mother! Mother? Oh, what do you think! It's happened, happened to me! All the way back on the train I could hardly keep still, I don't know what the other passengers must've thought, but I wouldn't be ladylike. Mother! Come and look. Do I look different? I must look different, I feel as though I've swallowed a firework. Oh it was a lovely, lovely c̣ɩy. We took a picnic, climbed up to the Waterloo Memorial, sat in the sunshine and it was after we'd finished the egg and cress; he couldn't wait till after the fruit cake! I felt so – shy, suddenly – I had to just stare and stare at the tablecloth while he was asking, blue and yellow squares, there was an ant struggling to carry a piece of cress across the corner . . . These are things you remember all your life, I suppose. I didn't think it would be like this. (*Pause.*) And then we just ran and ran! Talked, made plans, I felt somehow – weedy! (*Laughs.*) – Sort of silly, for having given in . . . to – love! – Do you know what I mean? (*Silence.*) Mother? We ate your fruit cake on the train, Jack put a paper down so as not to drop crumbs on the velvet upholstery, but then he sat on a strawberry – and oh, I got a grass stain on my frock, but Jack says he'll buy me a new one. *And,* Mother, *and* I got promoted to Head of Infants this morning! Miss Butterworth called me into her office, my heart was in my mouth, I thought she was going to tick me off for this dress being too short! . . . Jack was very proud when I told him, but of course he says I shan't need to work when we're – when we're – oh, of course he's going to ask you first, he's waiting in the front room, I opened the curtains so the neighbours can see – Oh and – (*Lights begin to fade.*) I've seen just the posy, tiny white flowers, in the window of Ambleton's . . . Oh Mother, I'm so happy, SO HAPPY! I suppose, really and truly, this is the beginning of my life! (*Lights fade to a single spot on* DORIS, *then snap out.*)

Solution to the Solitaire Game

For Rosie in Act Three, Scene Seven.

A Solitaire board (see diagram) looks much like a round wooden bread board, with a groove running round just inside the rim where discarded marbles are put. There are thirty-three holes on the board. Initially these are all filled with marbles except for the centre hole which is empty. The game is to clear the board leaving one marble in the centre hole. The rule is that a marble can only be moved by hopping it over another marble, up or down or across but not diagonally. The static marble which has been hopped over, is then removed from its hole and discarded.

For the scene, Rosie only needs the last eleven marbles on the board. She can then pace the final moves through the scene with Doris. There are no numbers on a Solitaire board, but the diagram opposite has been numbered for clarity. As can be seen, the following holes have marbles in them: five, nine, eleven, fifteen, seventeen, nineteen, twenty-one, twenty-two, twenty-four, twenty-six, twenty-seven.

The ten moves are as follows and each marble that is hopped over is removed from the board, while the hopping marble lands in a new hole.

1. Marble from *twenty-one* jumps over marble in *twenty-two* and into hole *twenty-three*
2. Marble from *twenty-seven* jumps over marble in *twenty-six* and into hole *twenty-five*
3. Marble from *twenty-four* jumps over marble in *twenty-three* and into hole *twenty-two*
4. Marble from *twenty-two* jumps over marble in *fifteen* and into hole *eight*
5. Marble from *eight* jumps over marble in *nine* and into hole *ten*
6. Marble from *ten* jumps over marble in *eleven* and into hole *twelve*
7. Marble from *twelve* jumps over marble in *nineteen* and into hole *twenty-six*
8. Marble from *twenty-six* jumps over marble in *twenty-five* and into hole *twenty-four*
9. Marble from *twenty-four* jumps over marble in *seventeen* and into hole *ten*
10. Marble from *five* jumps over marble in *ten* and into hole *seventeen*

The marble for the third move (from hole twenty-four), continues hopping through the next six moves. Therefore, when Rosie says 'double jump' or 'triple jump', what she is doing is playing the third to seventh moves as a sequence. The actress can delay picking up the hopped over marbles each time so as to prolong these moves. The stage directions indicate (*She removes a marble.*) every so often, as a rough guide. The actress can pace it as she wants, and add extra marbles if she wants more moves. At the point Doris leaves Rosie with the letter, Rosie should have four marbles left on the board, ready for the eighth, ninth and tenth moves. These are the moves with which Rosie completes the game alone and ends with one marble in the centre hole – seventeen. Solitaire!

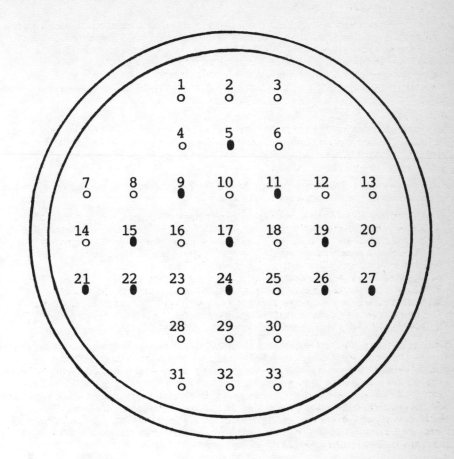